MARY,
WAYFARER

A CHAPEL HILL BOOK

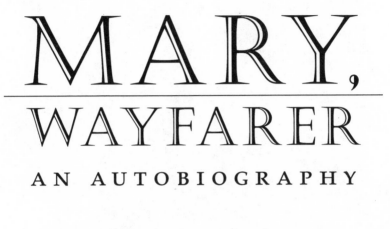

MARY, WAYFARER

AN AUTOBIOGRAPHY

Mary E. Mebane

The University of North Carolina Press
Chapel Hill & London

Copyright © 1976, 1983 by Mary Elizabeth Mebane
All rights reserved
Manufactured in the United States of America
First published by The University of North Carolina Press in 1999
Published by arrangement with Viking Penguin,
a division of Penguin Putnam Inc.
The paper in this book meets the guidelines for permanence and
durability of the Committee on Production Guidelines for Book Longevity
of the Council on Library Resources.

Library of Congress Cataloging-in-Publication Data
Mebane, Mary E., 1933–
Mary, wayfarer : an autobiography / by Mary E. Mebane.
p.   cm.   "A Chapel Hill book."
Originally published: New York: Viking Press, 1983.
ISBN 0-8078-4822-0 (pbk.: alk. paper)
1. Mebane, Mary E., 1933–   .   2. Afro-American women—North Carolina—
Biography.   3. Afro-Americans—North Carolina—Biography.   4. North
Carolina—Biography.   5. Afro-American women authors—Biography.   6. Afro-
American women college teachers—North Carolina—Biography.   7. Afro-
American women college teachers—South Carolina—Biography.   I. Title.
E185.93.N6M42   1998
975.6'00496073'092—dc21   98-46858
[b]   CIP

03 02 01 00 99   5 4 3 2 1

My story is real, but names and a few unimportant details have been
changed to protect the identity of people involved.—M. E. M.

To Harrison E. Salisbury,
a rock in a weary land

And I heard the voice of the Lord, saying,
Whom shall I send, and who will go for us?
Then I said, Here am I; send me.

—Isaiah 6 : 8

Part

ONE

1

Late in the summer of 1955, shortly after the Supreme Court ruled segregated schools unconstitutional (1954) and while the Montgomery Bus Boycott was still going on and a few weeks after Governor Luther H. Hodges of North Carolina went on statewide television to urge the black citizens of his state to accept something he called "voluntary segregation," I finally found a teaching job. (It is a historical irony that five years later the Governor became a member of the cabinet of the then most aggressive civil rights president in modern times, John F. Kennedy.) My job was in Martin County, North Carolina, in a place called Robersonville.

To get to Robersonville from Durham you go first to Raleigh, then change for a local bus going east. After you leave Raleigh, with its gray concrete five- or six-story buildings, there are fields of low-growing tobacco plants and tall green spindles of corn. Field after endless field, some so large that the eye can follow them to the horizon. But most are just wide spaces within the landscape, so that if you open your eyes very wide you can take in the whole field at once.

The tobacco and corn make an interesting pattern, representing both a pleasure and a staple. The tobacco is low, the broad dull green leaves starting just a few inches up from the mud-brown fields. The leaves grow out horizontally, row neatly on top of row, a little ruffly around the edges. The tobacco plant grows up so far and then stops short, never really pointing toward the sun. The leaves are dull and do not reflect the light.

But the corn is a dark and shiny green, glistening when the sun strikes it. Its leaves are narrow and have sharp edges. Children used to put the small sharp leaves in their noses and make them come out of their mouths. Sometimes they came out with blood on them. Corn reaches up and up—taller than a tall man—and, unlike tobacco plants, never seems to want to stop growing.

You can use a tobacco leaf as a fan. But if you're not careful a corn leaf will cut you. It makes nasty cuts in the tender places between your fingers—especially the webby skin between thumb and forefinger.

People of the region eat cornbread. They eat it plain; or sometimes they cut a slab and fill it with a hunk of country butter; or they pour a flat plate of molasses and sop it up with cornbread. Cornbread can be made fancy, with fried pork rinds, called "cracklins," distributed through it. Cracklin bread is considered a delicacy and is plentiful only in cold weather, around hog-killing time. Cornbread can be a whole meal in itself. You can put great chunks of it in a mayonnaise jar full of ice-cold buttermilk and eat the results with a spoon. A glass of buttermilk, a piece of cornbread, and a piece of fatback meat fried hard is a noontime meal anywhere in the region.

Ever since I was a child, the church has preached against tobacco, but gently. Sometimes the preacher himself would take a "chaw." A "chaw" is a piece of chewing tobacco—tobacco that has been pressed together and seasoned to make a hard pack. Men were fond of taking a wad of chewing tobacco early in the morning, forcing it into the back of the mouth where it formed a lump and sat all day mixing with saliva. They frequently spat and shifted it around a bit to get more flavor. In some public places there were shiny vessels called spittoons

4

placed on the floor in strategic areas. Plain folk used a metal can to spit in, one that once had held tomatoes or pork and beans.

Another favorite form of tobacco was snuff. Snuff was tobacco finely ground to a powder and seasoned. Some liked it sweet and some liked it dry. Railroad Mills Sweet was a favorite of Nonnie Mebane, my mother. Women mostly "dipped" it. Dipping snuff consisted of filling your front lip full of the fine powder. Since you might not be able to stop work in the fields to refill often, you'd pack in as much as possible. Thus a dipper's mouth looked full and swollen. Sometimes women who were a little prouder than the others filled their back right or left jaws instead of the front lip; they always looked as if they had an advanced case of the mumps. Outdoors, dippers would spit great arcs of brown saliva; indoors, they kept spit cups by their chairs. The snuff turned the teeth yellow and stained the gums.

Though both men and women "chewed" and "dipped," it was mainly the men who chewed and mainly the women who dipped. Pipe smoking was more common then than cigarette smoking. Besides, cigarettes cost money; mainly city folk smoked them. Then, too, women who smoked cigarettes were considered "fast," which meant wise in the ways of the city and probably immoral.

So the two crops of the region grew side by side, and the people made their living from both; they got bread from the one and pleasure from the other. One was life and one was said to be death. In various towns in the state, tobacco was made into cigarettes, which were then shipped to all America and the world. The tobacco factories gave employment to thousands and made a handful of people rich. Some of the rich spent their money in the world's playgrounds; others gave some of their tobacco money to educational institutions and charitable organizations.

Whether the plants were tall or low, dull or shiny, broadleaved or narrow-leaved, the blacks worked on them all. Plowing in the fields with mule or tractor, from early morning until dark, bending over the tobacco, standing tall amid the corn, they worked—men and women and children.

The women had on patterned cotton dresses, faded from many washings. Occasionally one woman would wear a Sunday dress, too small or too worn to be used for Sunday anymore. It would be shiny and of a solid color, sometimes with a big rhinestone pin permanently sewn on the front. The women often wore aprons with pockets to keep things in. They wore shoes but no stockings—the dirt cut up stockings too bad. Some wore huge straw hats, called "sundowners," which put their faces in shadow to the nose. Still others tied their heads with scarves.

The head scarf was draped in a triangle, slightly uneven if it was a large scarf. The fullest part was placed at the back, narrowing on the sides and tied in the front by the little ends. Then everything loose was tucked under.

Often the women were very black from the sun, and their faces gleamed like metal.

Sometimes they were slim—from the bending, stooping, and pulling. But those who had worked for a long time in the fields grew stout from the overuse of some muscles and the nonuse of others.

The men wore overalls and long-sleeved shirts to protect themselves from the sun. They wore heavy shoes called "brogans" or "brogues." On their heads were straw hats, sometimes with pieces missing where they had been grasped too often when fanning away flies. Some men preferred cloth caps with long bibs that threw their faces in shadow.

In the fields the laborers' movements were so skilled and deliberate that, if you passed by on a bus and looked out, for a moment you might think that you were looking at a painting. The field workers were figures frozen in time and place, like "The Reapers."

The blacks were not bending over their own fields. If there was a white frame house near the edge of the fields, set back from the road, large and well kept, recently painted, and fully underpinned, the owner was white and the blacks were his tenants, or "hands." If the house was large but unpainted, and if there were farming utilities sticking out from under it, the owner was white but not very well off; he was a working farmer himself, farming on shares with the blacks.

The blacks' houses were usually close to the road: a patch of bare brown yard, an unpainted shack with the front porch boards buckling up, the front door open so that you could see right into the house. Those children too young to work in the fields played in the yard, with an older one to look after them. Often they would stop and stare at whatever was passing by on the road. They too looked like a painting: frozen in motion in a bare yard in front of an unpainted shack with the door open and a clothesline across the front porch. Eyes large and clear, their skin a smooth black, they paused in their endless activity to look at what was new that had pierced their world.

Sometimes a short, skinny TV antenna hugged the chimney of a shack—that was ironic. These people seemed to be frozen in time, but they weren't. The mid-twentieth century had invaded even the most primitive dwelling. It brought news of the world beyond to all who could see or listen. And sometimes—even in the most sluggish personality—something clicked, glimpsing possibilities unknown before.

The highway bus would roll smoothly past painting after painting of rural America, the Southern United States. The bus was tuned to the mid-twentieth century, unheeding the hands in the fields, the large white houses that looked "tight" against the weather, the large unpainted houses where some white farmer was striving desperately to avoid sinking into the poverty faced by his poor tenants in the unpainted shacks with the wondering children in the yard. Low green plants, tall green plants, wild vegetation, houses against the blue sky—the mid-twentieth century rolled right past them.

The bus—shiny metal, hard, gleaming, symbol of an efficient technological age—would catch the sun and streak through the landscape. One had the feeling that the country could go up in smoke; wars, revolutions, famine, and pestilence could devastate mankind; people could live and people

7

could die, people could love and people could hate; but the highway bus would roll on inexorably toward a destination that was always receding—just a little farther on.

The highway bus would pass the pastoral scenes and then abruptly it was passing the Baptist church—nearing a little town. The church had spires and a glass-enclosed square black box on the lawn telling what the sermon had been or would be. There was also a graveyard. The flowers from the last visitors had withered or had been beaten down in the mud by rain, and the ribbons dragged the ground.

The bus wouldn't glance at the names; it was in a hurry. Just ahead were the gasoline pumps. The service stations were among the most modern structures in the town; they served the mid-twentieth century. They were like the bus: clean, efficient, gleaming, designed to fill one function over and over, without beginning and without end. Sometimes the bus pulled up at one of them—it didn't matter which one, as they were all indistinguishable—and took on packages and passengers or left packages and passengers. Then it started up again, passing the Methodist church, somewhat smaller than the Baptist church, the five-and-ten-cent store, the A&P, the local dry goods stores. And then that little town was past and the bus hurried on to the next one, driving through identical pastoral scenes to reach it: fields, "hands," houses.

The bus seldom passed the police station or the jail—these were hidden off on a side street. Deep in the psyche of the community, these structures were not available to just any eye for observation. Leftovers from another century, they were shy of showing their faces in the mid-twentieth century. So the bus would roll on past them, unseeing and uncaring, but the jail was there and so were the men whose job it was to keep it filled. The "hands" knew it was there. It had been built mainly for them. Just as the police existed mainly for them— to keep the blacks in line. Religion and commerce were the smiling face of the town, but at its heart was repression.

Wendell. Zebulon. Nashville, N.C. Parmalee. The towns flashed by. There were fields, then spires and a graveyard, and service stations and shops and fields again, and on and on until the bus pulled to a stop in front of a service station and the driver announced "Robersonville," while the "white" taxicab pulled up closer to the bus station and the "black" taxicab followed a little behind him. They were reminders of the recent past, when the "white" taxicabs carried only white passengers and the "black" taxicabs carried only black passengers. Now, in 1955, both white and black vied for what passengers they could get, because most of the travelers, black and white, were being met by their relatives and friends in cars.

I got off in Robersonville. I picked up my hard beige suitcase tied around the middle with a heavy yellow cord and my long shoulder bag and the remains of my lunch in a crumpled paper bag, and slowly made my way down the aisle. I walked slowly because I didn't want to get off. I didn't want to be in Robersonville at all. I had wanted to go to graduate school and get a master's degree. I had studied and passed all my courses with honors at North Carolina College at Durham, and had won the coveted *summa cum laude*—but to no avail. My peers got scholarships and fellowships and even Fulbrights abroad, but I had come to a little town in the eastern part of the state to teach ninth-grade English. Riding past fields and "hands" and little churches, I'd had to smile wryly at fate and to wonder when and how I could beat the odds. I had beat one set of odds, only to look up and see another one ranged against me. Would the battle ever be over?

The taxi let me out on Second Street, in front of an old house with peeling gray paint. I was heartsick, but I wouldn't let that thought rise to the surface. Is this what I had endured the four years of drudgery at North Carolina College at Durham for? I had gotten up very early every morning in the Wildwood community in Durham County, early enough to catch a ride with the factory workers who had to be on the job

in Durham by seven. I always left home by six-thirty, sometimes earlier. I took my lunch. In the four years that I was at
the college, I never once set foot in the dining hall, for I didn't
have the price of a meal. Then there was a two-mile walk
home from the bus line in the dark, for there was no one to
pick me up and the bus line stopped in Braggtown, far from
Wildwood, where I lived with my mother and my niece. But I
persevered, for if I didn't there was nothing in this world for
me to do. Blacks couldn't get jobs doing much of anything,
not in the five-and-ten, not in department stores, not for the
telephone company, not anything. The American South had
shut me out of the job market. Still, my options were better
than those of most black girls in the segregated South, for I
had been born in a tobacco town and could have gone to work
in the factories. But even that work was fast drying up; I had
heard my mother talk of machines coming and of "hands" let
go.

(Though the "machine age" had entered the Liggett and
Myers tobacco factory during my mother's long tenure there,
still I was shocked and surprised when, on a visit to Durham
in February of 1981, I heard that the factory had been sold and
that there was talk of moving it from Durham altogether.
Durham without Liggett and Myers just wasn't Durham anymore to me.)

There were also jobs to be had at a teaching hospital in the
town, connected with Duke University, but I had heard of
whole cadres of black workers there being fired when they
protested job conditions and wages. So in the solid segregated
American South, I knew that I had to become a professional or
work in factories or kitchens, public or private, for the rest of
my life. The South was structured that way, to keep at the
bottom a pool of unskilled, low-paid workers.

My landlady in Robersonville was Mrs. Welles, a smiling
black woman with a scarf on her head, who resented my four
years in college, for she herself was still substitute teaching on
a tenth-grade high-school certificate. Mrs. Welles had a curious sense of status. She often referred to the fact that her fa-

ther had not been a field slave—that his job had consisted of helping "the mistress" around the house, and "picking up apples—nothing hard." (In other words, he was a house slave.) She told me about her father's duties on any number of occasions, looking in my face as if to get confirmation from me that her father's occupation did indeed make his daughter's pedigree superior to that of her peers—now nearly all dead—those whose fathers had been field slaves. I would stare blankly back, giving no sign.

I had reason to recall these conversations in the early sixties, when Malcolm X came to speak at my hometown, Durham, and made the key point of his attack on the black bourgeoisie this distinction between field slaves and house slaves. Only his priorities were different from Mrs. Welles's. In Malcolm's schema, the field slaves were the true revolutionaries among the blacks and the house slaves the appeasers. How you view history depends a great deal on your vantage point.

Still, Mrs. Welles seemed friendly enough, spoke well, and fixed delicious meals.

Robersonville was a little larger than most of the eastern towns. It had a weekly newspaper—a tabloid with a black-bordered section in the back headed "Colored News." One of the first issues that I saw ran a picture of the new school under this heading. The school could barely be seen through the knee-high grass that the photographer had shot through. There was an inset picture of the principal, looking like a wild man.

(Southern white papers took a fiendish delight in distorting the features of any black's picture that they felt obliged to run. Nobody looked like himself—never better, always worse. A favorite shot of a black in the Durham papers was of a suspect glaring from his caged cell. And the first time that I saw a photograph of a black on the front page of the Durham *Morning Herald*, it was that of a mother who was not yet ten years old.)

In Robersonville, downtown was roughly a block and a half, dominated on one end by Rose's five-and-ten-cent store.

11

Rose's was nice; I loved to browse there. The counters were piled high with fresh goods. The soft goods had bright colors, and the hard goods were shiny.

There were plates with bold designs of dark red flowers and deep green leaves; they looked as though a child had painted them. There were solid-color cups and saucers and bowls; my favorite color was a chocolate brown with a mottled beige trim. These dishes were heavy and wouldn't break as easily as the thinner white ones with the pale pink-and-silver flower design. There were piles of gleaming forks, knives, and spoons. Cookie cutters, sieves, can openers, gelatin molds, dessert dishes, crystal bowls, flower vases—all spilled in profusion. All America, through an intricate process, had gathered together this abundance from all the states and some foreign countries, had had it brought by ship, plane, train, and truck, and had dumped it in Rose's five-and-ten-cent store in Robersonville, a little town in an isolated sector of a Southern state, where farmers and merchants, tenants, and landlords came to look, sometimes to buy, and sometimes to ask shamefacedly what an unusual-looking item was used for.

The dresses at the store looked fresh, but they were very sheer. A dress from Rose's needed a good petticoat, because it was sheerer than the dresses in the higher-price stores. That is probably why the wearers starched them—so that they would hold up through more than one wearing and one washing before they started looking bedraggled. But they were pretty—bright pink, yellow, and green prints for warm weather, often edged with white piping on the sleeves and collars. For cold weather the dresses were solid colors: sturdier fabrics of pink, yellow, and green, with a multicolored scarf for trimming.

Farmers came to town on Saturday, the end of the week: he, she, and the little ones. When they all left, they would be carrying packages from Rose's: he, underpants; she, a flowered Sunday hat; the little girl, a bright-colored gingham dress; and the baby, a toy that he would break in the car before he got home.

The local clothing stores might consider themselves more

high-class and charge twice as much, but Rose's had the customers.

On the other end of the block was the bank, and, in between, the United States Post Office, hard by the movie house and a few stores.

Two main arteries emptied into Main Street, which ran from east to west. One north/south street, First Street, led to the "high-class" black section; the other north/south street, Second Street, ran past the poor black section of the town. On either street it was easy to tell when you were in a black neighborhood: the pavement stopped. On Second Street, the pavement ran a little way down the street, then stopped abruptly. The dirt signaled the beginning of the black neighborhood—that and the fact that the railroad tracks became fully visible there also, running out from behind some buildings and continuing parallel to the street for several blocks until they curved out of sight. Houses of respectable but poor blacks faced this street. Their owners hadn't yet made it one block farther over to First Street, where the high school principal and the undertaker lived.

On First Street, though the pavement continued farther, there was a sudden falling-off in the general air of prosperity as one neared the black section from Main Street. The houses on First Street were mixed. The prosperous-looking ones shared the street with smaller, though carefully painted, houses. Some of these houses were well kept, but others had lawns that did not have store-bought grass; often the window and door screens bulged where the young ones had pushed them out with their hands.

Zoning regulations were not enforced in black neighborhoods. Therefore, on First Street, not far from the principal's house, was the neighborhood "juke joint." It was noisy, and music constantly floated out onto the street. Men, full of beer, stumbled on the steps. The voices coming out from it were sometimes happy and sometimes angry—always boisterous.

First and Second streets ended in another east/west street, at the eastern end of which was a school. On the western end was a church, and between the school and the church were several blocks of teeming black folk. Here lived those who had never had a grip on the "good" life and couldn't care less, along with those who had not yet quite "made it" and regretted it very much. On this street were "shotgun houses." They were called that because the rooms were boxed one behind the other, and it was said that if you stood in the street and fired a load of shot through the front door, it would go straight through the door of every room until it went out the back door. In such houses privacy was impossible.

There was also a little section of five or six houses near the black school, all grouped together facing each other. It resembled an African village, teeming with life at all hours of the day and night. Closer to the church the houses got better, with some older residents holding on to the home place, fixing it up and holding their heads high, though their neighbors were not of the highest status.

Next to Mrs. Welles's house on Second Street was a modern brick house, whose side porch faced a path that led to First Street. The front faced Second Street, but it might as well not have, for no one ever entered or left by the front of the house. There were no lights on at night in the house, and during the day the curtains, a flimsy white, hung still, as though no activity at all took place in the house. But it was occupied. Mrs. Welles opened her storehouse of information and revealed that the occupant of the house was named Lila. She was a cripple and had been a schoolteacher. The house had been built for her by her brother, a prosperous landowner. They were "people of means." He had built it so that she would have a place to go, somewhere to hide, for she had decided to shun the company of people. Her life had not turned out the way she wanted, and for that she hated her mother. She was a polio victim and walked with a pronounced limp. Her handicap had not prevented her from completing college and returning home to teach elementary school. But someone had inflicted an emotional wound on her, and, whether it was that one wound or whether it was a succession of wounds, she had found that she couldn't endure people anymore. So she shut herself up in her brother's house and came out only when Robersonville was asleep.

I spotted her once in the early morning dark. For some reason she was walking on the railroad tracks. She had on a pale yellow cotton dress with ruffles on the bodice. She herself was pale yellow, with long black hair. The two us stared at each other in silence—I on Mrs. Welles's porch and Lila on the railroad tracks. We both seemed to be caught in a spell. The world was silent and barely dark, barely light. We both could have been at the beginning of time.

Then something happened to break the spell. I suspect that I involuntarily looked down for the Raleigh *News and Observer*, then moved away; the figure in the pale yellow dress turned into a frightened, wounded creature and scampered away, dragging her wounded leg.

I empathized with Lila and wanted to go next door and introduce myself, so that we could talk and, perhaps, get to be friends. But I never saw Lila again.

I sometimes walked along the streets of Robersonville, though I didn't like to. I was afraid once I got out of the black neighborhood, which one did in a twinkling. That was the surprising thing to me in really small country towns: lines of demarcation between black and white neighborhoods were truncated, so that before you could take one deep breath you had passed the dividing line and you were walking in a white neighborhood. Riding in a car wasn't so bad. In a car one felt more protected, shielded against what was viewed as a hostile, threatening environment.

In my walks about the town I dreaded to pass one house. It was not the same general dread that I felt in passing through white neighborhoods—it was particular. The house was large, but not unusual-looking. In fact, it looked like a large rooming house. It was a frame structure, two stories high, glistening white, and it had a square, boxlike shape. In the front someone had added two long columns, probably thinking they would give the place elegance. They didn't. Instead they made

15

the square, ungraceful house look squat. It was set back from the street, but not far back, for the lot it was on wasn't very deep. Close under a window there was a tall tree that reached up to the second floor.

The blacks in Robersonville said that the "hanging judge" lived there. The judge was white, and the blacks felt that he hated them, and gave those convicted the maximum sentences. He kept to his house, which the blacks passed daily, going to and from the main shopping district. I used to look up at the faceless windows of the house, and sometimes I imagined that I saw him standing at the window, wearing a dark frock coat, looking out at the blacks.

One summer in Durham, when the Bookmobile came to Wildwood, I had checked out *Native Son*. I knew well the feeling that Bigger must have had as he moved across Chicago from the black neighborhood to the white. It was a feeling of danger.

This feeling sharply emerged in one of my early walks around Robersonville. I came upon a little white structure, curtained and with venetian blinds. Though it was a warm day, the door was closed. But through the curtains I could see white people within. A tiny sign said "Library." I paused. A library in Robersonville? Perhaps it wouldn't be so bad after all—teaching down here. The school library had few books, and those in it were mainly for student readers. I had been desperate for books since I had come, missing the Bookmobile and the black public library in Durham and the rental library in Baldwin's. So this little spot was a relief. But something stayed me. This little sign said, "Library," but perhaps it was a private lending library. Ought I ask? Yes? No? I debated with myself a few seconds, then moved on. It seemed forbidden.

Without access to books, and uninterested in the talk of the people around me, I made my way in Robersonville as best I could. So this was to be my new life. *Why not you?* a voice said. *Others have come and have stayed, built homes and made stable lives*

16

for themselves. What makes you think that you're so much different from anybody else? Why are you so ambitious?

And I felt guilty that I did want more. There was a great big world out there, and I wanted to be part of it. There were high places to attain, and I wanted to attain them. Why not me? Why not me? If not here, maybe in New York City; if not in New York City, maybe Paris? Somewhere there's got to be a *way out*. Why not me?

"Because it is vanity," said the church. "Because it is arrogance," said my peers. "Because it means you're getting beyond your raising," said my family. But, I thought, who is it that has ordained my place in life? Who has any right to tell me who I am, what I must do, what I must think, how I must view the world? I won't listen to anybody but me.

"All right, hardhead," the warning said. "You won't listen and you are going to be sorry. Then don't come running to me crying. I told you. Hard head makes sore back."

"That's all right," I said. "I'll take the consequences. Whatever the consequences are, I'll take them. I'm going to see what life holds for me."

I shook my head to shut off the tapes, the tapes that had been made so long ago and continued to be made over and over again—by parents, and peers, and others who came in contact with me. They always said the same thing: "Be satisfied. Be happy. Why do you want more? Who are you to want more?"

I blinked my eyes and looked out in front of me at my class, my reason for being.

They needed teaching, and I had come to teach them. But I was ill-prepared to teach them. Nothing in my methods class had taught me what to do when one half of the class stays out one day and the other half stays out the second day. There were only about five regulars in my classes. Their parents were economically stable enough so that the children didn't have to work in the fields, either for their own families or for somebody else. The other children were not that fortunate. This was the eastern part of the state, the soybean- and peanut- and tobacco-growing part. In the fall the harvests were ripe, and the "hands" were recruited from the entire black population. So the black children stayed out of school to harvest crops—most often for the same white landowners their parents worked for.

The white superintendent of schools cooperated with the white landowners and put the black schools on half-day schedule so that those who did persist in going to school would still be out early enough to work seven or eight hours a day in the fields.

But he didn't put the white schools on half-day schedules. The white landowners didn't want *their* children to miss school and fall behind.

Thus as I traveled across the state on my way back to Durham on Friday afternoons, I could see black children working in the fields. The white children I couldn't see, because they were behind the glass windowpanes of their schools. But their school buses were in the yards, so I knew that they were still inside. In county after county, the scene was the same: an ethos in the region that said it was all right to deny blacks schooling, but not the whites. After all, weren't the whites preparing for tomorrow? And tomorrow would be just like today. The blacks would be poorly prepared and would thus have to work for the whites, who would be better prepared. The blacks were under and were going to stay under, and their main way out—education—was going to be abrogated or denied them altogether.

I looked at my students. They had so much talent, talent that was to be forever lost. The world would never hear Zeno sing. A shy, quiet person, Zeno had perfect pitch. I had read about perfect pitch but had never known anyone with it. One day I was leading choir practice, one of my many duties, and I went to strike a tone on the piano, but Zeno sang it for me instead. Then I tested him and found that he could sing tone after tone on demand—without getting his bearings from other notes. I was excited; there in the little town of Robersonville, I had in my class a genuinely talented young man who would

18

go far in life, who would become one of the world's great operatic tenors. I talked after school to him about my dream. But I hadn't gotten to him in time. His parents, peers, and the racially unjust society in which he lived had already been at work, and he did not have a high concept of himself, of what was possible in his life, and my talk of an operatic career was just as foreign to him as the notion of his walking on the moon. He listened politely, but I knew that he didn't even hear me. Ah, Zeno.

There was also fragile-looking Lola, who wore flowers in her hair and could make even the inexpensive clothes that she wore look fashionable. She could have been a fashion designer or a buyer. But at fifteen, life had gotten to her too. She would probably get pregnant before she was eighteen and marry and help her husband make a living at whatever it was that they would do for a living for the rest of her life. She would send her little Lolas to school, where they would follow a route similar to hers.

So I talked about nouns and verbs to people who had been in the fields yesterday and would be in the fields tomorrow, and who would be in the fields the rest of their lives. Some of the boys would grow up to go into the Army to help America fight her wars, and the girls would marry and have children and work in the substratum of society that America had reserved for them. If the girls didn't marry, they would still have children; the black culture forced them to—to prove that they were women. And life would go on, and I would be sitting in the classroom twenty years from now teaching the children of these children, who would have the same fate as their parents unless something was done.

As I sat at my desk, the Trailways bus passed by my window. The road was lower than the surrounding terrain, which was overgrown with tall grass. Thus the bus seemed to be swimming through the underbrush. And I longed to be on it.

So I wrote letter after letter after letter. They drifted down like rain on offices in New York City. Even the oil companies who had schools in Saudi Arabia got some. But when I sent in

19

my vita with my photograph on it and they saw that I was black, they didn't write back.

Then there was the answer I received from Accra, Ghana, which said that they were not recruiting teachers from overseas without a master's degree. And I despaired.

But I continued to write letters. I imagined an enormous chute stretching from Robersonville to New York City; I put a letter in on my end and it came out on the other.

The heat of late August faded into a clear September. The days were all the same. I grew used to seeing the seats in my classroom empty day after day. I followed the principal's instructions and kept two class rolls: one for the principal, which listed accurately the staggering number of absentees; the other to be turned in to the state as the official roll, showing an acceptable level of absences. Eighty percent, the principal explained, was an acceptable attendance figure. Since attendance was actually fifty percent or below, I had to learn fast how to falsify figures. If the attendance rate wasn't high enough, the state would cut the number of teachers alloted to the school. Into that cynical situation, the black principals had interjected the law of survival: falsify the attendance figures. I hated to play the game, but I had to admit the logic of it. It was then that I learned how corrupt systems make people become corrupt in order to fight them successfully.

So I taught and raised money. East End was a brand-new school, but the county wouldn't spend any money to equip it. The black school administration was of course dealing with a white superintendent. (A favorite story was that once a black male teacher shook his hand, whereupon the superintendent took out a large handkerchief and carefully and with great deliberation wiped his hand.) Clearly we wanted to stay in his good graces, so it was decided not to pester the superintendent for needed equipment; the teachers would raise the money instead. So day after day I found myself selling slices of sweet potato pie that somebody's mother had baked and donated to the school. Or I myself brought rolls and wieners and onions and mustard and helped my classes fix and sell hot dogs. Or the students sold chances on a cake to be given away at Friday's assembly. Sometimes, as a result of these activities, my class netted all of five dollars for the week. Week after week some of my colleagues reported fifteen dollars, or even twenty dollars. I wondered how they could do it, for I begged the children just as hard as I could to bring money, but the plain truth was that they didn't have it to bring. Then I figured it out. My colleagues were contributing from their own pockets to the drive.

Across town, my white counterpart had no such pressures. She could teach her pupils whatever subject she had been trained in, and she had adequate equipment to work with. But eastern North Carolina thought that reading and writing were things that rural black boys and girls didn't really need.

I had heard black Baptists teach of retribution, of a reckoning day. I looked and looked for a sign, for something that would show me that this injustice would not go on forever. But I never saw any indication that God was looking or that He even cared.

I decided that at the end of the year I would go to New York City. I would look for meaning in life, for happiness, for peace of mind, for people who would like me. Some people said that I had talent; I would go to the big city and see. My life had to change. It had to get better, didn't it? Things didn't stay the same, did they?

But I hadn't yet gotten smart enough to know that external situations change in response to internal changes, not the other way around. Break the mold inside and sometimes you can force the outside to yield to your new vision. That knowledge of life, and of myself, was still in the future. But for now I was planning to flee north to a new life. However, I was really on a treadmill, something like a television news shot in which the film rolls behind the newscaster, giving the impression that he is moving when in reality he is sitting still.

I moved from Mrs. Welles's house, and the million questions she asked, to Mrs. Williams's house. She had a son in my ninth-grade English class, a nonlearner. A more sophisticated woman would have seen the ploy from the beginning, but I didn't. I genuinely believed Mrs. Williams when she called me up one night and commented in a friendly way on a choir program that I had presented. When she saw me downtown and had been most friendly, I was very happy. At last I had a friend in this godforsaken town. So I gladly left Mrs. Welles and moved to a tiny house with Mrs. Williams and her three children. We laughed and talked and sat together around the television set. Then I didn't go home every weekend, for Mrs. Williams was nice to me. In all the friendliness, I failed to see that little Willie was supposed to pass the ninth grade because his teacher was friendly with his mother. Little Willie didn't pass, and I lost a friend, but I gained a new knowledge of the world.

Still, my stay with Mrs. Williams was not without its bright spots. Mrs. Williams loved to tell stories about the neighbors, most of whom I didn't know. But the stories were interesting. One of them was so stark in its simplicity that I have never been able to forget it: Mother and son were close; then he married, and the mother hated his wife. When he left to go north to find work, the mother bombarded him with a steady stream of letters containing derogatory information about the wife. The son came home and, after an all-night argument, killed his wife and himself. He looked angry in his coffin. To me the story had an air of inevitability, like a Greek tragedy.

Another east Carolina story, equally stark, was this: A black woman forsook her black lover for a white lover. One Sunday morning the jilted lover waited patiently in the yard of a country church until the service was over. Then he shot her as she left the sanctuary; she fell dying on the church steps. Informed of what had happened, the white lover tracked the black one down and shot and killed him, then disappeared from the county, never to be seen or heard from again.

I saw the church where this had happened one Sunday morning, on my way to some little eastern North Carolina town. It was a white painted structure, set back from the highway in a dirt yard, like thousands of such structures all over the South. As I watched, I seemed to see the participants in the story act their roles out.

It was after I moved in with Mrs. Williams that I met Mrs. Madison, an elementary-school teacher. She was the object of considerable talk in Robersonville because she sent all her clothing to the dry cleaners—every item, excepting lingerie. A schoolgirl came to her house every day after school to wash Mrs. Madison's underclothes and stockings. People said that this was an extravagance, and who was she to do such things? After I got to know her, she told me her story. Her family had lived in a small town that had a small white college: she, her mother, and her siblings. To keep them alive, her mother took in washing from the college. Every day her mother kept one of them out of school to help her do the wash. So Mrs. Madison never went a whole week to school. Then every night her mother ironed, and she expected and got the help of her children. So night after night Mrs. Madison ironed. Even if she went to school in the day, at night she helped her mother, along with the other children. This routine proved to be so taxing for the growing girl, and she was so unhappy about the schoolwork she was missing, that she swore that if she ever got in a position to do so, she would never ever wash another piece, and she didn't. I wondered how many of Mrs. Madison's detractors knew her story and had experienced similar hardships. Would they have been so harsh in their judgment if they had?

One day in Robersonville, in Martin County, North Carolina, I saw Nefertiti. Jet-black, she had on an unadorned deep yellow dress and was seated at the wheel of her car with the door open; thus, I saw her in profile. It was the same woman that I had seen in an art book. Nefertiti had survived thousands of years and had made her reappearance in this unlikely place. I wondered how many of the residents of Martin County knew whom they had among them and appreciated her beauty.

While I was teaching in Martin County I observed a bus situation very similar to one that I had seen on a Durham city bus in the early 1950s. In Durham the driver had threatened a black passenger with arrest; this time, however, the outcome was different. One Sunday afternoon, as usual, I boarded the bus going back to Robersonville. The bus was traveling to Elizabeth City, North Carolina. It was a sun-splashed afternoon, rather warm, and the bus was not too crowded. I was sitting idly, thinking about nothing in particular, when something caught my eye: it was the seating pattern on the bus. When it had first started loading, everyone sat by himself—all the way to the back. Then more passengers boarded, and soon all the whites had seat partners, but some of the blacks didn't.

Then a white man in a dark navy suit with lots of gold braid got on the bus. I remember thinking that he was probably on his way to Norfolk, Virginia, to the naval base there, and I wondered why an officer would be riding the bus. But something was happening. The officer didn't sit down; he was standing, right beside an empty seat. Sitting on the other side, near the window, was a black woman in a gray blazer, her hair in a shoulder-length pageboy, and the officer didn't want to sit beside her. Everyone settled back, the Navy man remained standing, and I waited to see what would happen. This was 1956, a year after the Montgomery Bus Boycott, and shortly after the Interstate Commerce Commission had passed a ruling that banned segregation on interstate carriers. So segregation on buses was under attack and crumbling, but not yet completely.

The bus driver quickly scanned the bus; he then took his seat and started backing out. The Navy man stood very erect, his suit without a flaw or wrinkle. The woman with the pageboy and the gray blazer looked down at her lap, as if reading something. The bus entered the street; the man still stood; I waited to see. Norfolk was a long way from Raleigh. Finally, the bus cleared the city and got on the highway. At that point the Navy man sat down. No one had said a word.

May came and with it the end of school. It was my first year in my new profession and all in all I hadn't done badly. I hadn't been able to teach what I had prepared for, but I had started to learn something of the ways of the world.

2

It was a June morning in 1956 when I blinked my eyes on the Turnpike. The bus had left Washington, D.C., at four a.m., and when I could no longer see lights from far-off towns and villages, and there were just the Christmas-tree lights of tractor trailers and interstate buses, I had fallen asleep. Now in the gray morning I stirred in my seat and looked at the other passengers, heads lolling and mouths open, still asleep. Everyone blissfully trusted the skill and wakefulness of the bus driver, who alone was awake and aware.

But just as the gray monotony of the landscape and the whooshing tires started lulling me to sleep again, I jerked up with a start. Far in the distance was the fabulous place, the city that was the Mecca for America's provincials and a second home for American blacks.

If you were to ask the first ten blacks that you met in New York City, "Quick now, where are you from?" six of them would answer Georgia, South Carolina, or North Carolina. One or more of them would deny Southern origins, and the others actually would be from New York City or some other part of the country. Black Virginians hardly ever migrated to New York City, contenting themselves with the metropolis of Washington, D.C.

There were so many Southern migrants in the City because it had long been presented to black Southerners as the Promised Land, a place where there were no segregation laws insulting and humiliating you at every turn, a place where you could make big money. So they came, from every nook and cranny of the South, often arriving in winter clothes in the summer or summer clothes in the winter, with beige striped suitcases tied with string because the catches were broken. Whole families came, the men in overalls and felt hats, the women in dark crepe dresses and patent-leather shoes, the children in long socks and tie-up shoes. This was to be their new home, the place where at long last they would know a sense of freedom.

And though the North often disappointed them, the promise was still there, and they came.

I longed to go to the City, mainly because the City offered me escape and shelter. In the City, I would be able to go my own way, without being coerced by the preindividualistic group to which I belonged. No one would try to force me to conform, and perhaps in that way I would be able to find out who I really was and what my mission in life was, since I had not been able to discern that so far. Perhaps in an environment where society had fewer shackles, fewer means of pressing one down, I could find a place for myself. That is what I wanted most of all. *A place.*

The City looked hazy blue in the early morning dusk. It looked miles away, almost like the sky city that I used to imagine in the clouds that floated overhead, when we were out in the fields at home. I nodded and awoke, nodded and awoke, and each time the spires grew taller and more distinct. Skyscrapers, twentieth-century cathedrals.

Suddenly the sunshine was lost in the darkness of the tunnel; then there was the artificial light of the Port Authority Bus Terminal, and I was there. Here in the City I would see if life couldn't have more meaning.

I had saved some money, and now I was starting a new life. On Monday morning I went to look for a job. I went to the offices of America's leading magazines and newspapers. There was no interest in my application.

In the afternoon I went to a giant insurance company, the one my mother believed in so much. She felt that it would never go out of business. All of our insurance in Durham was with this company. The afternoon was a repeat of the morning. There were no jobs to be had. The ad in the paper? Oh, that job has already been filled.

I decided to learn the skills of the City, so I enrolled in a business school in Manhattan. From my window I could look out at the lions guarding the New York Public Library, which was my home during lunch hour. After school I headed for the movie house. There in the dark, icy quiet I saw film after film. Every day I went to the movies. One day, playing on the same bill with the film that I wanted to see was another film. It had titles at the bottom of the screen. At first I was startled, for I had never seen a foreign film that hadn't been dubbed into English. This was something new, so I decided to sit through it. It was about a young man who seduced a circus performer and that night went to see her act at the circus and taunted her. I thought that it was a very cruel movie, but it was different in that people talked a lot about things in the film. It was not all action, but some discussion as well. I was seeing a different view of the world and that was what interested me—something different, another interpretation of human life.

Later in the week I read a review of the movie. The critic discussed at length the filmmaker—Ingmar Bergman. It was the first time that movie criticism had any meaning for me. Heretofore I had depended on the newspaper to tell me what was playing, who was playing in it, and what the story was about. Now I began to realize that the critic could serve some other function as well.

My days flowed into each other. Classes until the afternoon; then the movies; shorthand practice at night.

Something put it into my head that I could be a writer. So I got the Columbia University catalog and found a course in creative writing. You could enroll only with the permission of the instructor. I found the instructor and asked him if I could be in his class. He was a youngish man, sort of brown all over, with a sallow complexion and dark brown hair slicked at an angle across his forehead; he wore a tan suit with a coat, even though it was summertime. I sat right by his desk and told him I wanted to be a writer. He looked up at me, a bit startled. He asked me if I had ever written before, and I told him no. Then he sat and tapped on his desk blotter with his pencil about ten times and told me that it was all right, I could come to his class. I knew a wild joy. I was in New York City and I was going to learn how to write stories and novels. I would say good-bye to Wildwood and the frustrations of teaching. I would become a writer.

Class the first night was dominated by a woman in an enormous straw hat. She sounded like a Midwesterner and looked like a staunch pioneer type. The instructor tried to tell us about markets and publishers and other things that I had never heard of, but he was constantly interrupted by this lady, who evidently feared silence. During his discussion he talked of what distinguishes an artist from other people. For an example, he used the actor and the circus performer in the Ingmar Bergman film that I had recently seen. I was startled, for movies had never been a part of classroom discussion where I came from. Yet here at Columbia, they were relating something showing down on Forty-second Street to life in the classroom.

One woman was Hispanic, from the Caribbean, and she talked about her many servants and how she wanted to write about one in particular—"a very strong, but loving man." I took a deep breath and said nothing. I felt that I was out of my depth. On the way home, in the subway, one member of the class, a perspiring stocky woman with thick dark hair, sat beside me, asked me a few questions, then started telling me about her novel and her agent and how she was in advertising and how she was nearly through with her second novel. "Second novel," I said to myself. "I'm in a class with someone who has already written a novel! I can't possibly compete in this class; I'd better drop out." I thought about it on the long ride to Brooklyn. Still I was undecided. I wanted very much to stay in the class, for I wanted to learn the techniques of writing, but how could I possibly compete with these people? I thought about it for a day or two.

Then, after the second meeting, I decided to drop the course and get my money back. The dark-haired woman told me her name, and I remembered it for a long time, for I wanted to read her book when it appeared. But it never appeared. I should have learned a lesson from that experience—that people have been known to exaggerate. But I still had far to go in learning the ways of the world.

Soon I was running low on money. Evening classes were less expensive. I figured out that if I went to evening classes, I could practice in the daytime and could also see more sights of the City. So I transferred.

I lived in a rooming house in Brooklyn, in the low 400s on Quincy Street. One morning something happened there.

It had taken a long time for me to become aware of it, but something was wrong about the sounds of the voices I heard in the background. I couldn't tell where they were coming from, whether they were children playing, or adults, or what. I went to my third-floor window and looked out on the street. A slim black woman and an equally slim black man were standing on the sidewalk in front of one of the row houses. I couldn't tell whether it was the third house or the fourth down from where I lived because it was on the same side. The woman on the sidewalk was saying things up to somebody who answered from the third floor. But I couldn't see, so I really couldn't be sure. The first thing I thought when I saw them was, "Why aren't they at work?" It was the middle of the day. "My Southern outlook," I said to myself. In Wildwood in Durham County, North Carolina, adults worked during the day.

As I listened, I could tell that there were bad words being exchanged, but I couldn't make them out clearly for I stood back from the window to keep the participants from seeing me. Then something flashed in the sun, and the woman on the sidewalk grabbed her face. She didn't move at first.

"You could have put her eye out," the man called up to the

other woman. Another object crashed, glancing off the woman onto the ground, and he started leading the woman away. I could see blood coming down under her fingers where she had her hand across her eye. I surmised that the woman who was hurt was the wife, or steady girlfriend, that she had come to confront her rival and, failing to get in, had resorted to shouting from the sidewalk to make her feelings known, and that her rival had responded by throwing a water glass down on her.

What most struck me, though, was the way the injured woman and her male companion reacted. They walked slowly, deliberately, to the bus stop on the corner; they did not hail a taxi, they did not act as if it were an emergency situation. I was in panic. Horrified. Maybe the woman had been blinded or, at the very least, scarred for life. Yet this terrible thing that had happened to her was being treated in a most casual way by everybody concerned. Was the City the cause? For a long time afterward I wondered about her. Was she blinded? How did she feel that such a calamity happened and no one, not even she herself, regarded her as important enough to care?

The girl in the room next door was named Francine. She was a dark, chubby girl, very pretty and full of life. I didn't understand her private life, though. She was married but separated, she said. However, on occasion her husband visited her. He was a very dark man, with a muscular build. I met him once by the railing. He would visit Francine, and before he left I would hear them on the bed. I wondered why they had separated, since they got along so well, but Francine never commented and I never asked. Francine also had a boyfriend. He was a lighter brown and rather short. He visited her very often and I would hear them in her room, too.

One night I left my door open, because the bedroom was stifling. Suddenly a man darted out of Francine's room and ran under the creamy light of the skylight down the stairs. It was the boyfriend. At the same time I heard the heavy tread of a man's footsteps on the stairs. In a few moments the husband's head appeared near the foot of the banister. I was scared to death. I wondered if he had seen the boyfriend, for there was only one way out. And if he had seen him, would he be mad and come in and beat Francine or maybe kill her? But I heard no commotion, and I never heard the door slam downstairs, indicating that the boyfriend had left. I wondered how the husband had got in. He had not rung the bell. But maybe he had a key; or maybe one of the tenants had let him in, for it was summer and many people lounged about downstairs. At any rate I was afraid for Francine.

The husband went into Francine's room, and after a while I heard them. Then he left. I went to the kitchen at the end of the hall. As I was returning, I saw the boyfriend standing on the stair looking through the banister. "Is he gone?" he asked. I said, "Yes." He smiled and sort of winked at me and slipped into Francine's room. He had been hiding all that time in the bathroom on the second floor.

I thought that I'd better move.

The sign in the window said "Room," so I decided to inquire. The house was pleasant-looking enough, considering the neighborhood, in another part of Brooklyn.

I rang the doorbell and a man about twenty-five years old answered the door. I wondered what he was doing at home in the middle of a working day, but decided that perhaps he worked at night. Besides, it wasn't any of my business.

He invited me in, looking at me with interest, but cautiously, as though he didn't want anyone to see him looking.

I entered the narrow hallway and went through the door on the left, the landlady's rooms. The young man followed me in.

The landlady was a stocky brown lady of indeterminate age, rather nice-looking.

"I'm looking for a room," I said.

"Where are you living now?" she asked.

I didn't respond to that.

The landlady looked a little puzzled at me and said, "Where are you from?"

I wanted to ask, "Does it show?" but decided against it. "I'm from the South," I said. My standard reply.

The landlady looked interested and said, "Oh, yeah. Where from?"

"I'm from Durham," I said.

"Oh, yes, I know where that is," she said. "I was born in Wendell, not far from Raleigh, and Raleigh is not far from Durham."

She became a little friendlier after that. But one part of me still observed the man. He was nice-looking, with curly hair that sprang up from his smooth brown face, and a smooth mustache. He was sprawled carelessly in a chair, his muscled chest revealed under a short-sleeved, open-necked dark blue sweater. His gray pants were too tight, showing finely muscled legs. His legs were splayed open. I wondered who he was and what role he played in the house. Was he a relative, son, cousin, what? I couldn't be sure, but I decided against "relative." I had noticed that the landlady was sitting with her dress "high." And black women don't sit with their dresses high around male relatives. It is around males that they wish to attract that they sometimes adopt this posture.

To sit with one's dress high means to sit so that an interested observer can look up a long expanse of inner thigh, sometimes as far as the woman's underpants, if she has any on. Mothers who want their daughters to be virgins when they marry often warn them about sitting high. A standard admonishment is, "Put your legs down, girl. One of these days, you're going to put them up and won't be able to get them down." They never say what it is that will prevent the girls' putting them down—too modest. They mean that a man will be between them, and, what's worse, the resulting baby will be born when their legs are up and open.

"You can have a room, provided you abide by my rules and regulations," the landlady was saying.

I was a bit startled, but more amused. I had been busy noticing and commenting to myself on the landlady's posture and its probable meaning and the role of the young man in the house. I had been thinking, So this is the City, when I learned that the landlady had rules.

"Oh, what are they?" I couldn't help the little laugh that bubbled out around the sides of my question.

The landlady crimped her mouth and put her legs together.

"Your boyfriend can visit you here, but he'll have to leave before day."

"Leave before day?" I inquired.

The landlady was embarrassed. She hadn't been away from home too long to know that the standard that she was setting would have been unthinkable in the rural, churchgoing South, where if an unmarried woman had sexual contact with a man, "respectable" people pretended that it had never happened. Such things are not done.

Nevertheless, she persevered. "I mean, don't let him stay all night."

I uttered a weak, "All right." I wanted to get out of the room before my laughter exploded, which it did as the landlady preceded me up the steps to the third-floor bedroom.

One day as I passed my neighbor's door, I noticed that it was open slightly, and I glanced inside involuntarily. I passed by, then took a step back to make sure I had seen what I thought I had seen.

A woman was half lying, half sitting on a bed. She was a large, yellow, middle-aged woman. Though it was the middle of the day, she hadn't dressed yet. She had on a petticoat which rode up on her large, lumpy legs. She had one bare foot tucked under the other. This position forced her legs apart, showing an enormous patch of bushy hair. The sun was high and was throwing a yellow streak on the floor. The woman seemed quite content as she studied the cards she was holding up close to her chest.

At the foot of the bed, half sitting, half lying, was an aging "pretty man."

A "pretty man" in the black community is more an attitude than a "look," though looks do play a part. He can be light-

33

skinned or dark-skinned, but he looks smooth and polished, as though he has never shaved at all. Dark areas showing razor burn usually take a man out of the pretty man class; as a matter of fact, other signs of mature manhood are taboo for him also. A pretty man cultivates a boyish image. He doesn't have frown lines, never wrinkles his brows in a furrow, never looks grim-faced, serious, or stern. Such looks frequently are associated with responsibility, and a pretty man doesn't have or plan to take on responsibility of any kind. He plans to remain a boy forever. And it is this tender, smooth-skinned, babyish person that he presents to the black woman who, because she has no one, often turns to him, giving him presents to keep him coming back, paying the rent for him, and often subsidizing him in other ways as well. He can live and thrive among the blacks because there simply are not enough men to go around in the black community.

The pretty man that I saw looked too old to be playing his role; he was about forty. But she was at least fifteen years older, so perhaps she was still glad to get him.

As I watched, he selected a card and threw it down on the bed. She picked it up and chuckled as cigarette smoke curled from her mouth. Neither he nor she exhibited any sign that there was anything untoward about the situation. If she knew that I had paused, fixed by the scene, she gave no sign of it. On a sunshiny morning in a Brooklyn tenement, life was going on.

One night, even though it was midnight, it was hot. The City held heat so much that sundown brought no relief.

I was walking through Tompkins Park, coming home from a concert at the Lewisohn Stadium, where I had sat on ice-hard stone steps and listened to glorious live music, conducted by a miniature man about a mile away. Once I got off the subway, my way led through the park. It was dark and shadowy, with patches of moonlight and lamplight splattered on the grass and walk. Couples lay in embrace right out in the open. They had deserted their hot closed rooms for the hot open space of the park. Though it was late, I wasn't afraid. I didn't mind walking in the City; there were streetlights everywhere, and even this late at night there were people about. At home in Durham, in my home community of Wildwood, I hated to walk at night, even though many a night I had walked the long distance from the bus line home when I was a student at North Carolina College in Durham. There were no streetlights in Wildwood, and you had to walk in the dark if it wasn't a moonlit night. In a way, I preferred a dark night—it made me less visible. On moonlit nights hostile dogs could see me coming no matter how softly I walked. And cars with male occupants could spot me at a greater distance. The City was less scary.

I walked along, still lifted up from the concert, when I heard the music of a guitar and the running feet and laughter of children. I wondered about it, but not worriedly, for it was a happy sound. Then I heard singing and looked up to see a horde of children following in the wake of a slender black man, about twenty years old, who was singing and playing the guitar. The children were everywhere, so many of them that they spilled far over on the grass and formed a long triangle behind him. There were boys and girls, teenagers and pre-teens, and some adults, and they were laughing delightedly. The guitar player seemed to be slightly apart from the group, yet not hostile to it. He was a modern pied piper.

He passed me, singing and picking his guitar, while a hundred children ran delightedly behind him.

I was fascinated and charmed by the scene. I laughed out loud as they passed. It has remained one of my happiest memories of the City.

One day I noticed that a room that had been closed was now open. Inside there was a lady sitting by the window. In spite of the taboo in the City against associating with strangers, I was lonely and dared risk speaking to her. In response to my timid knock at the half-open door, the lady looked around from the window and invited me in. I introduced myself as a new neighbor and said that I was from the South. The lady didn't seem much interested in the fact that she had a new neighbor, but she brightened somewhat at the mention of the South. She herself had come up from the South some years before and had remained in the City since. I looked around at the room. It was incredibly neat, with nothing out of place. Everything was in a container of some sort. In one corner was a huge bed, beautifully made up with a magnificent spread. The floor was smoothly waxed, the curtains freshly starched, and the tiny kitchen in the closet neatly ordered. The sheer orderliness of the room gave a sense of space and of quiet. But it also made the occupant's life seem unbearable—dreary and transient. It was Thursday afternoon and she was off from her housekeeping job on Long Island. She "slept in" and had Thursday afternoons and every other Sunday off. When she told me that she had lived in that room for fifteen years, I knew why the room depressed me so. That room was the lady's life. She came here on Thursday afternoons and every other Sunday to sit and not disturb anything. There were no paintings on the walls, no books, no magazines, not even a newspaper read and carelessly folded. There was nothing that said that a living, breathing person lived there.

I imagined that the lady came here and sat by the window in the afternoon. She probably had had lunch on the job or had eaten in the City. Maybe she had seen an early movie. In the evening about dusk, she probably went to the spotless kitchen and fixed a modest supper. She wouldn't have reason to fix a large one, for she would be gone tomorrow and the leftovers would go to waste. I wondered what her supper would be. Perhaps Vienna sausage or canned salmon; she would open the can, then wash and neatly store it, to be taken down and placed in the garbage as she left on her way back to work the next morning. Perhaps she would have some canned peas and a piece of fresh fruit that she had gone into the street to buy when the vendors yelled up. Then she would go to bed and early tomorrow morning she would go back to her job, where she would suspend life again for another week, then come into the City on Thursday afternoon again and sit by the window.

Life has got to mean more than this, I felt. It has to.

It was a Saturday night, and the bus had the artificial brightness of buses and subway trains in New York. It made a lot of noise as it lurched along the crowded Brooklyn streets, avoiding double-parked cars and careening taxis. The driver was white; most of the passengers were black.

The bus passed rows of houses, situated close to dark, littered streets. In some of the houses people sat in lighted windows with the shades up. In other houses all of the windows were dark, as if the inhabitants were away or gone to sleep.

The bottom of the corner house was always well lit, though. That was where the bar was, and clusters of men spilled out of the bar onto the sidewalk and into the street. Most of them just stood, but some leaned against the nearest parked car.

The driver stopped at one bar and a passenger entered. He was a black man around thirty, not tall, and a little husky. He had a felt hat on and an old coat that looked like the coats sold by the Salvation Army.

But around his neck he had a magnificent guitar. It gleamed in the artificial light. The passenger plunked his money in the token box, took a seat right behind the driver, carefully arranged his guitar, and said to the driver, "You don't mind a little music, do you? It's Saturday night and a little music won't hurt nobody." With that he burst into rapid strumming and loud song. The driver's face was a study, but after one brief glance he drove on. The other passengers looked on, indifferently big-cityish. At first I was mortified at the unconventional behavior of the passenger, but after seeing his face, then the driver's, then the other passengers', I leaned my head against the window to control my laughing.

The bus rolled on, the man kept picking and singing at the top of his voice, and the other passengers acted as though they were not affected at all.

My people in the City, I thought.

One day I decided to look at typewriters. I went to a rental agency just across Fifth Avenue from the school. I entered a store which was little more than a narrow, well-lighted aisle. Someone had entered almost at the same time that I did. I sensed that it was a man, but I didn't really pay any attention.

"Do you have second-hand typewriters for sale?" I asked.

The clerk was a middle-aged white man, with square, shining glasses. He looked as if he had not been out of the City all summer. He looked at me, then beyond me at whoever had entered when I did.

"Can I help you, sir?" He directed his question around me at the other person.

"Oh, by all means wait on the beautiful lady first."

The man's voice was educated and foreign. I heard him, but wondered whom he was talking about, for there was no one in the store except the three of us. I looked around for the beautiful lady, wondering where she was. I noticed that the clerk was looking around too. Then it occurred to both the clerk and me at the same time that the "beautiful lady" was me.

In a secret, very deep part of me I was greatly moved. I looked at the man who had said this. He looked Mediterranean, except that he was tall. He was rather husky and had thick iron-gray hair. I ventured to look in his face, wondering what I would see, but he didn't seem adventuresome. He looked quite everyday, in a pin-striped gray suit on a hot muggy New York afternoon. He looked as if the observation he had just made about me was self-evident to anybody. I was so mixed up I didn't know what to do. What kind of world was this, where I have to wait until I am in New York City and a stranger from some faraway country looks at me and sees beauty, when my countryman, the white storekeeper, hadn't seen it, and, what was even more devastating, I myself had never thought of myself as a beauty? What kind of society had produced the clerk and me?

I walked the city streets and smiled at children; rode the subway and found it interesting to speculate on the heritage, personalities, and goals in life of the incredibly varied men and women who leaned over me, completely unseeing, absorbed in their newspapers. I wandered in the park, never really getting used to so much cement, watching the graceful skill of city children bouncing their balls against tall concrete barricades that evidently existed for no other reason than to have balls bounced against them.

On the weekend I escaped to my favorite spot in the City, the garden of the Museum of Modern Art. I watched the crowds of people wandering there and liked to give them histories and personalities and aims in life.

In peddlers' stalls on Ninth Avenue were some of the biggest tomatoes that I had ever seen. Tomatoes didn't grow that large at home. I used to stop at stands throughout the city and look at the odd and beautiful produce that was on sale. That was one thing I liked about New York. You could see odd and unusual things there.

I used to go to "Garden City" on the upper West Side every day and buy a fish. They had an enormous counter beautifully arranged with all sorts of fish, most of which I had never seen back home. I loved fish, having had it nearly every Friday for as long as I could remember: mullets, croakers, butterfish, porgies.

But here in Garden City I saw some varieties I was unaware of: bluish-looking fish; reddish-looking fish; big fish like the ones people catch and hold up, grinning, while someone takes their picture. So every day I would stop and buy one fish. Except Saturday. Then I would buy two—one for Sunday.

Near Garden City was an open-air market where white men with ruddy skin and black hair shouted rude remarks at each other and laughed while they waited on the customers. I liked to shop there. They reminded me of the way black people laughed and talked to each other in the South. The stand held tomatoes called "beefsteak" tomatoes and one day, after an especially friendly conversation with the clerk, I had asked him where they came from. I didn't know what answer I expected—probably California. A faraway, rather romantic place. I was rather disappointed when he said, "Jersey." New Yorkers always said "Jersey," never New Jersey.

I was startled again. New Jersey was not that far away from North Carolina, but it grew a different variety of tomato from North Carolina.

The days passed and my typing improved. One day I went down to take the New York State Employees Examination. I waited around for the results and found that I had passed. I could type forty-five words per minute. I was offered a job on the Friday before Labor Day with the Multiple Sclerosis Foundation. I thought about it all weekend, for what concerned me was that my starting pay would be much less than I could make teaching. For that and other reasons I decided to give it up and go South again.

For one semester in the spring of 1957 I was the English teacher, librarian, choir director, and principal's secretary in a school in Pinehurst, North Carolina, one of the richest resort communities in the United States. What about Pinehurst? Well, the blacks lived in a little place a couple of miles away called Taylortown, and the police chief had "sent word" to all black women and girls that they were not to appear on the streets of Pinehurst in shorts. He evidently feared that they might attract the attention of wealthy white males. White women and girls, of course, could wear what attire they pleased. The black women did not challenge this invasion of one of their basic rights. There was a quiet murmuring, but no black woman wore shorts in Pinehurst, North Carolina. The time, as I said, was 1957.

I decided that this community, the playground of the white rich, was not for me. In September 1957 I went back to Durham, my home base, where I got a job teaching English and social studies at Whitted Junior High School.

3

"Attention all teachers. Attention all teachers. At the ringing of the bell, proceed in an orderly manner to the nearest exit. In an orderly manner. There is no cause for alarm."

The children gave a whoop of joy; there would be no classes for a while. I had to move quickly to keep them from stampeding.

The principal's voice on the intercom went away, and a second later the signal for the fire drill started. But it wasn't a fire drill. When the bomb scares had first started, they used to pretend that they were fire drills, but they had had so many that nobody bothered to pretend any more. For it was fall in the American South. And every fall brought with it headlines: TROOPS, FEDERAL MARSHALS, RIOTS, DISORDERS. In 1954 the Supreme Court of the United States had declared segregated schooling to be unequal schooling and had demanded that it be stopped "with all deliberate speed." But the South had said, "Never," had planned "massive resistance," and the headlines were the result. For in the fall of 1957 schools were still almost totally segregated in the South and would remain so until the 1970s. What was causing the headlines was the entrance of a handful of black children into schools with an ocean of white children. The black children often were menaced by white parents, harassed by their white teachers, and abused by their white classmates. Some whites protested the presence of blacks in "white" schools by threatening to blow up the black schools and kill all the black children.

In the fall it was not at all unusual to find oneself standing

41

among happy black children in the bright sunshine on the lawn of a public school while white males in dark blue police uniforms searched for bombs, room by room, locker by locker. If they found none, they went away and the children stomped reluctantly inside. Sometimes the bomb scare came so late in the day that the search would take the rest of the school day, and the children went home early, delighted.

One such scare occurred on a Friday afternoon, before I had had time to gather up the materials I needed to take home for weekend work. So while the dark blue uniforms searched my room and the children's lockers right outside my door, looking for explosives, I sat calmly at my desk, searching through my papers. To a stranger from an alien planet, or maybe to a human being from another time, another place, this scene would have been one of pure madness. But this was the American South and insane events took place so often that they had the air of the commonplace.

Some people advocated something called "peaceful change" in the South. To me the phrase "peaceful change" was a contradiction in terms. Change means pain; it also means violence. To wrench anything out of its accustomed course takes energy, effort, and pain. It does great violence to the existing pattern. Many people want change, various types of change, both in the external world and in their own internal world, but they are unwilling to undergo the severe hurt, the incredible pain that must precede it.

The only peaceful change is surface change—powdery snow blowing off the ice-hard earth.

I have read that rivers in extremely cold climates freeze over in winter. In the spring, when they thaw, the sound of the ice cracking is an incredibly violent sound. The more extensive and severe the freeze, the more thunderous the thaw. Yet, at the end of the cracking, breaking, violent period, the river is open, life-giving, life-carrying. No one says, "Let's not suffer all the violence of the thaw; let's keep the freeze; at least everything is quiet then, unmoving, unchanging." No, after the winter is over, when it is time, people want change; they want the ice to melt and are willing to endure the violence that accompanies it.

Some blacks wanted change and they were determined to have it. Segregation and discrimination were the deep and extensive freezing over of the minds, bodies, and psyches of the people of the American South. When the climate was right, the thaw set it. It was accompanied by violence. Public schools were bombed; churches, meeting places for civil rights activity, went up in flames; people were wounded or killed.

Children in a Sunday school in Birmingham were mangled by bombs while they studied "The Love That Forgives." Klansmen in Mississippi killed three young men named Goodman, Schwerner, and Chaney. They knew the young men were civil-rights workers because two were white and one was black. They represented change, and their violent death was the result of change.

When the thaw set in, I was in an eighth-grade classroom, frozen, fixed, unable to get out; when it ended, my life had a radically new pattern. Without the change in the social order—and change in myself—nothing would have been different. Everything would have been the *same*. And the *same* was dreariness beyond belief.

I never knew what went on in the building between three-fifteen p.m. and three-thirty p.m. because I was at my desk or out in the hall solving such major crises as "I lost my shoes."

"How could you lose your shoes?"

"I don't know."

"You don't know. You walk around with no shoes on and you don't know when you lost them?"

"Yes, ma'am."

"Think now, when did your feet get cold?" A little humor sometimes helped.

The upstairs hall near the principal's office in the spring was a sight to be seen. On display were all the lost items that had never been called for: boots, raincoats, caps, scarves, sweaters, expensive eyeglasses, and other personal effects.

Tired of the conversation about the shoes, I suggested that he look in his locker again, and I turned to solve another dispute.

"He's talking about my Mama."

"What did he say?"

"He's talking about her."

"Well, what did he say?"

"He's signifying."

"Where do you live, Son?" I liked to affect "Son" with the boys. It made me feel older and wiser than they were.

"On Crest Street."

"Where does he live?"

"McDougald Terrace."

"That's clear across town from you. How can he know your Mama? Are you relatives? I'll bet he's never even seen your Mama."

I had scored a telling point. The aggrieved one acknowledged it by turning from me. But he had lost a battle, not the war.

"Just you wait," he yelled to his tormentor. "I'll get you outside."

I sighed, "Oh, my." But "outside" was the job of the teachers on bus duty; let them worry about it.

I also settled scuffles at the lockers and kept in talkers and those who didn't know their spelling words. Talkers had to write "I will not talk" a hundred time and poor spellers had to write the words they missed ten times each. It never failed to amaze me that students whom I had forgotten about during the whirl of the day's activities would show up to take their punishment. "What are you doing here?" I'd say.

"You told me to stay in."

"Oh, well, come on in then." And gladly would they troop in, spirits bubbling. Some of them came so regularly they'd have a paper, "I will not talk," already filled—their friends had helped them write it at recess. If I saw it, I'd confiscate it and make them write the sentences again; otherwise, their little hearts would be made glad—they had put one over on the teacher.

By that time the teachers' bell, which gave them permission to leave, had been sounded at least ten minutes. I would then go upstairs around three-forty-five to sign out and get any official forms—they flowed from the principal like rain—then go back downstairs, read and respond to the forms, see to it that all balled-up paper was cleaned out from under the desks—the students always crumpled paper into little balls— see that the windows were closed and that the shades were even near the center where the top and lower sashes met. This activity—evening the shades—was crucial. The principal commented on its importance at staff meeting. Then I would catch my breath for the first time that day.

I would review the incredible events of the day. I generally arrived at the school at eight a.m., because experience had taught me to get the jump on the students. It helped a little; when I got there, there were only two or three students—usually those who had to come farthest—outside my door, room 8–6.

In a few minutes in would come flying braids and skinny, flashing legs—"Sinclair's gone to the store!" This was a major crisis. Whitted Junior High School faced a busy intersection right where the street divided: in front, the school; on the left, a snack shop. Children who had gotten out and walked to a bus stop and then had taken public transportation to school, sometimes five miles or more, were expected to proceed directly to the school, not go to the store. The teachers were expected to be in their classrooms, keeping the children from tearing down the walls brick by brick; in the halls, preventing personality clashes that sometimes ended with a punch; and out on the street, keeping Johnny from buying salted peanuts and a Pepsi—all at the same time. This was madness.

"So Sinclair's going to the store." I did not say it out loud, but thought, Well, hooray for Sinclair. I secretly wished that Sinclair would stay in the store—then maybe I'd have a little peace, at least for that day.

Next came the jangle of lockers being slammed and greetings exchanged, while I stood halfway in the room and halfway in the hall, keeping an eye on everybody.

I tried to look at each student as he or she entered the door, noticing expressions, wondering what kind of environment each had come from, knowing from experience that some of their living conditions were unspeakably bad.

It was the policy of the Durham city school system to have every teacher visit the home of each child in her homeroom. That was before large-scale integration. The policy was discontinued after integration—the blacks said that the whites didn't want white teachers to go to black peoples' homes.

This was a policy I liked. For one thing, it taught me the various sections of the city. I had been raised in the county and, except for the main thoroughfares, I knew little about the black sections. And any new experience, no matter what, was a joy. So I bought a city map, located the streets, and after church on Sunday made three or four house calls.

More important than the adventure was the knowledge I gained of the circumstances in which my students lived. Some lived in what appeared to be stable environments, others amid disorder or chaos. I once visited the home of a very quiet young boy in the early afternoon. Every adult in the house was drunk and noisy. He alone sat calmly and talked with me.

The principal had once told me, "Miss Mebane, I give you the problem boys because you never hurt their feelings." What happened to *my* feelings wasn't his concern.

There had been relatively little integration, so that black students from all over the city came to the centrally located junior high school: children of faculty members at the black North Carolina College at Durham, and of the black professional classes; sons and daughters of tobacco factory workers; children of nonacademic employees at Duke University; and children from the alleys. I used to muse that such a mixture of students should be an example of democracy in action. How wrong I was.

Students from middle-class homes expected and often got special treatment, both from their peers and from the teachers. The principal did what he could to break up this practice, but he never fully succeeded.

I taught my class in a tiny dark room in the basement. Half of the room was below ground level. The yard sloped in front. Where the slope was sharp, I could look out level with the grass and see the wheels of cars. Above the slope in the other half of the room I could see only the retaining wall—no sky. I knew when the sun was shining because of the sheen on the grass. If the sun went in, the grass looked grayish-blue and lifeless, like artificial grass.

The room was cramped and close. The seats were jammed closely together, with a narrow sliver of aisle between them. There was a slightly larger path around the room. The radiator was on the ceiling amid a tangle of plumbing pipes, which often clanged ominously. The only clear spaces were squares on either side of my desk. In this tiny, dark, claustrophobic room were jammed more than thirty-five students—when they were all present.

The eight-thirty bell sounded, and lockers slammed and students cascaded into the room.

First came devotion. There was no getting around it. One must have devotion. It was in the Manual. I would ask one of the students to sing a song: "My Country 'Tis of Thee," "This Land Is Your Land"—they particularly liked that—and someone would lead the Lord's Prayer. I disliked singing religious songs, having felt ever since I myself was in school that religion was a private matter and that teachers didn't have any business trying to teach it.

We were past the Lord's Prayer and then came the Pledge of Allegiance. I wondered if any of the students felt the irony at hearing the words "with liberty and justice for all."

Next I called the roll and filled out absentee forms. If a student was absent three days in a row, I had to call or visit his home.

But time was passing and I had to hurry, for today was Bank Day. Once a week, to teach the children thrift, the local black bank encouraged the children to bank nickels and dimes. I thought it was a good idea, but there was no time for it. It would have been so much easier if banking had been done at Activity Period. I had to hurry and send the money up or the principal would be on the intercom demanding it. Again I had to hurry and read any announcements. These were in addition to the ones given over the intercom by the principal. Bell. Class change. Oh, my!

Next, I was supposed to start English and social studies. But, naturally, some of the homeroom activities carried over into the beginning class period, and if I was a little bit late sending the class absences up to the office, the intercom spoke. If a student came in after the roll had been called, a frequent occurrence, I had to drop everything and rush up the stairs to the office to change my report. Tired and out of breath, I'd rush back down to start the class, a third of the period already gone.

Then there was another bell, and it was time for social studies, a subject that I had not been trained to teach. North Carolina history, required by the state, was anathema to me; it was insulting to blacks. I didn't understand why somebody didn't complain. Among other things, the officially adopted text painted a bucolic picture of human slavery. One day I discovered in a box in the back of my room a set of books on black history by Dr. Benjamin Brawley, a respected black scholar. How or why they were there I was never able to determine. I started on a campaign to use the books. I approached the principal.

"No, Miss Mebane, we're supposed to teach North Carolina history."

"But the students don't know anything about their own culture."

"We're required by the state to teach North Carolina history."

"But I've got the books right in my room."

"I'm up here. I don't know what you're doing in your room."

I took his remark as a hint to do as I wished in my classroom and proceeded happily to distribute books at the beginning of the period and take them up at the end. That month the students got a grade in North Carolina history, but they had spent their time reading something about black history.

After social studies came the bane of the classroom teacher, Activity Period—a time when students were supposed to attend clubs and other activities. Since few of them belonged to clubs, most of them stayed in that tiny room and fidgeted and talked—for forty-five minutes.

The library was so overcrowded that the librarian asked the teachers not to send more than a few students to the library at a time during Activity Period. I puzzled over the problem and decided to let the students go by rows: Row 1 on Monday, Row 2 on Tuesday, and so on through the week. I regretted that I couldn't take the whole class to the library.

Then came lunch period, during half of which every teacher had to stand in the playground or be on duty in the lunchroom. After my duty, I was so tired that I would go to my room, lock the door, and sit far back on the same side as the door so I couldn't be seen through the window, hiding from my students and anyone else who came to make demands on my time. This was the only break for the day.

Then the bell sounded, and a new set of students came in, exuberant from their full lunch break. There was a repetition of the morning's routine, and after two periods they departed, to be followed by a wild and woolly ninth-grade study-hall group. They came determined not to study *one thing*, and my day fell apart.

During each period, discipline problems have to be handled on the spot. For example, he's walking around the room and won't sit down? I get a pink card, write out the nature of the offense, give the card to him to take upstairs to the dean of men. In a few minutes he is back with a notation on his card: "I talked with him about his conduct." By this time another one is on his way upstairs with a pink card. In a few minutes he is back. What's the use?

Then at the end of the day I went into the hall to break up fights; solve problems at the lockers, such as the boys caressing the girls in strategic places—most of the time with the girls' encouragement, until they were spotted; saw to it that the desks were straight; kept students in; stumbled exhausted to my car; drove to my home in Wildwood, where I lived with my mother, Nonnie, and my niece, Diane. I would collapse on the bed and stay there until the six-thirty news came on and brought me back to life. After the news went off, I would get up and work on school papers until late. I would wake up in the morning praying, "Please God, let it be Saturday."

Sometimes I would lie in bed and wonder what could I do for my students.

Ed was sent to me straight from reform school. Shy, faint smile, terrible biography; his mother was an alcoholic who eventually abandoned him. By the time he was ten, he was sleeping in doorways. Later he was sent to a reform school for breaking and entering. He was restless, not a bad boy, not a dull boy. But I had no training, no tools to reach him. At Christmas, after school closed for the holidays, I sent my students Christmas cards through the mail. I never forgot the look on Ed's face when he came up to me after the Christmas vacation and exclaimed, "I got your card!" His eyes held real joy, and I knew that mine had been his only card.

Then one fine day the principal's daughter, Charlene, who was in the ninth grade, came by my room.

"Is Ed here?"

"No, Ed didn't come today. Is there a message?"

"No, ma'am." And she went away, leaving me wondering about her and the reform-school boy. How would it turn out?

A few days later, the principal called me in for a Big Conference.

"Miss Mebane, as much as I hated to, I had to suspend Ed. You know there are some people you just can't help. We've given Ed a fair try, but he's not trying to make it."

I smiled a wry smile.

I realized that talkers were seldom real problems, and believed that they talked so much because they were so full of drive and energy that was not absorbed by the dullness of the school's routines. They were never the dull students, who, for whatever reason, were numb to what was going on around them; nor had their energy turned to destructiveness. They were still within the system, a system that was not serving them well.

Ruth was one such student—bright, ebullient, with a full mouth, eyes set wide apart, sort of raw-boned, but not big. She had a ready laugh, and the boys liked her a lot. Lillie, her dear buddy, was bright, super-skinny. Once they started passing notes and I intercepted one. That was a quality about me that my students could never understand. How did I know so well when they were doing wrong? "Miss Mebane, you got eyes in the back of your head." I didn't know how or why, but I could look and say, "James, stop doing such and such," and I was always right. Later I figured out how I did it. Something about a person's face when it was normal—and his general posture—registered on my mind. When I looked up and noticed that the expression or the posture was different, I knew that something was the matter. The note that I intercepted had been sent by a boy to Ruth: "Let me do what I did to you at the locker yesterday." I thought of sending it to her grandmother, who had warned me that she was a bit "fast."

Many of the students lived with their grandparents while their parents—most often their mothers—went north to work. The grandparents often had to work too in order to support these children. Thus, the grandparents were a vital part of the family. I knew of examples in my community where people took care of, in succession, children, grandchildren, and others who were left for one reason or another with no one to care for them. Sometimes it was a relative; occasionally not. One day at church you might see a little boy or girl with a woman who would say, "The child has come to stay with us," and not much comment would be made after that first Sunday. Formal adoption papers were not necessary, and things generally seemed to work out all right.

I confiscated the note and said not a word.

That afternoon, Ruth came around to plead for her life. "Please don't send that letter to my grandmama. She'll give me a killing. Please, Miss Mebane, please."

"Ruth, I'll tell you what I'm going to do. I'm going to keep this letter in my pocketbook, and if I have any more trouble out of you this year, I'm not going to say a word, I'm going to send it to your grandmother."

"That's blackmail!"

"Take it or leave it."

Ruth took it, and the rest of the year when she got too ebullient, I would glance meaningfully at her and she would subside.

Ruth never knew that I had misplaced the letter almost as soon as I got it.

Then there was Benjamin. He was in the eighth grade, and couldn't read or write. Here was a boy in the city school system who had been passed from grade to grade and couldn't read or write.

The children teased him. One day I talked to the principal about him, and he spoke of the boy's "environment," as if that explained everything. Environment! What was he going to do for a living? One day Benjamin let me know he was aware of his predicament, too. He said, "Miss Mebane, people always say, you'll end up digging ditches. What's wrong with digging ditches? It's honest work. Somebody's got to dig them."

I started pointing out that machines dug faster and better, but I lost heart and never finished.

As one last measure I took Benjamin aside one day and asked him if he'd like to learn to read; I told him that if he'd stay after school I would try to teach him. He agreed.

I didn't know anything about teaching reading, but I would try.

I talked it over with the principal, who got me a first-grade reader. The lessons began. They lasted a week, and then he stopped coming. The children had found that Benjamin was staying after school to learn how to read, and he couldn't bear the teasing. Benjamin—what would become of him?

"Miss Mebane, I went home yesterday and my baby was dirty, and I told that woman who keeps my baby not to let him be dirty *any more*." Janet was talking. Janet was thirteen. She lived in a housing project; a teenage boy lived in the same housing project. Both of their mothers had jobs. Janet and the boy visited each other at night when their mothers were out. The result was inevitable.

Janet had wanted to come back to school, and the principal let her. I was nice to her, but I sensed that Janet was far older than I was. It was ironic, but it was so.

Then there was Clara, who stepped between her mother and stepfather as they were struggling over a gun. She pulled the trigger and he fell dead. She came to school even on the day of the funeral. I said nothing, but the children asked Clara about it right to her face.

What would become of Clara, what thoughts would she have at night, knowing that a man was dead because of her? What would be her thoughts ten years from now at twenty-three, at thirty-three, at forty-three? Would she ever know peace?

Lucy, a perfectly sculptured slim girl, had Carol by the hair.

"I know I've got him and she's trying to take him," she said, as I stood between her and Carol. I was taking licks from both of them.

They had picked the worst possible spot to fight over their friend Rene's older brother. Coal dust from the coal chute was all over them, and it soon got all over me, too.

I had to break it up; they were my students.

"I've got him, and I know I've got him."

"How do you know, Lucy?"

"I just know."

"But how?"

Her only response was, "No use her trying to take him. *I've got him.*"

They were women *so soon*.

Finally the day I was waiting for came: "Thank God, it's Saturday."

Saturday meant walking through stores, looking at the fresh and shiny things. For a few seconds I would imagine a workman bent over a bench in some far-off land, making the item, and for a brief second I drew a deep breath and was out of Durham.

Then the branch library awaited, with its polished floors and comfortable leather chairs. There the outside world awaited me in the bright, glossy covers of magazines.

I visited the world's capitals and fantasized that they knew and welcomed me there. Or I went to the theater, or astonished the great universities. When I had read the last magazine, which I usually lingered over as long as possible, I reluctantly left the library.

When, where, or how I would receive the further education that I desired so much, I didn't know. My staying at the head of my class at North Carolina College at Durham, eventually graduating *summa cum laude*, had meant nothing in my life. My blood family, as did Wildwood in general, had made known their view that since I already had a job teaching, I should now stop all the reading—for which I was notorious—and the striving. And certainly, most certainly, form an attachment with one of the black males around, and submerge myself among the black people there, and never look up during that long road between then and the grave. *I didn't see it that way.*

With my career stymied, blocked in every way, I couldn't do what most black Southerners do when things go wrong wherever they are—I couldn't find refuge at home. That was

and still is the saddest thing about my life—I didn't have a haven that I could flee to, where I could quietly lick my wounds
and gather up strength until I was ready to sally forth and do
battle with the world again. Most black Southerners venture
out—from the farm to the town or from Southern towns to
Northern cities—to seek excitement, adventure, another way
of life or whatever, knowing full well that if things start going
badly for them—they're in trouble, they're in debt, they've
lost in love, they're mixed up with the wrong crowd, they just
can't make it—they can always pack bags and boxes and head
south, and soon in some little, dry Southern town or desolate
farming community they will arrive at their destination, the
magic place called "home." Here there are folk called "people," and your people will slap you on the back, say they're
glad to see you, and set another plate and add another handful
to the pot. And you can rest a while until you decide what to
do, whether to stay or go back and try it again or try your luck
somewhere else. Then when you decide, you may leave again,
always knowing that you have a home and people.

But, instead of a place of refuge from the battle, my home
was the battlefield and the people there my principal adver-
saries.

Sometimes when I used to drive through Wildwood and
pass by our house I would look at it, wondering how it looked
to strangers, wondering how the whole community of Wildwood looked to someone who was just driving through, who
had turned off the main highway that led from town, the
highway that continued north on past other little communities—Little River, Bahama, Rougemont—on its way to Rox-
boro. To me Wildwood looked interesting. It was easy to tell
that the houses had been built at various times. Those that
had been built when blacks had little money, and banks and
other money-lending institutions refused to grant loans for
building, looked jerry-built. The owners had bought planks
and cinderblocks as they got the money, and they had impro-
vised the best they could. Sometimes a concrete porch would
go unpoured for years, or windows from an old or abandoned

house wouldn't quite match their new frames. But the houses built after World War II were built according to a plan, and, as the fifties progressed, became indistinguishable from the modest-sized houses in *House Beautiful*. The change interested me, I suppose, because I had known when there were only three or four houses in the whole community. Everything grew wild and was meant for picking: blackberries, pears, plums, scuppernongs, black grapes, locusts, creecy salad, black walnuts, hickory nuts, persimmons.

Though Wildwood had been built up, it still had an appealing atmosphere. In the spring everything became a green so intense that it looked artificial. Nearly every yard had a flowering bush, and in the spring after a rain Wildwood looked like a picture postcard.

Our yard bloomed, too. On either side of the driveway near the road were flowering bushes. Two had long curving slender branches drooping with tiny yellow flowers. One bush had branches laden with white buds. Deeper in the drive, near a whitewashed rock, was a lilac bush that had deep green leaves and perfectly formed bell-shaped lavender flowers. On the left, where the drive ended, was a huge wisteria vine, whose heavily scented dark and light purple flowers attracted every bee in the neighborhood. On the right, across from the wisteria, hard, fragrant, red wild roses grew all over a fence. On the left side of the house at the bottom of a little slope a row of buttercups that had been planted long ago still blossomed. There were many big shade trees on both the front lawn and in the back yard.

Our house had been built in the thirties; it was a five-room weather-beaten frame house that didn't look like a modest-sized house in *House Beautiful*. But my father had built it himself.

I don't know when the "bad" had first come into our house. It wasn't always there. At first our family was like most families in the community: father, mother, three children—two boys and one girl—and a relative: my father's sister, Josephine. The family functioned in a fairly normal way for the time. My father raised vegetables for the market and did odd jobs. My mother worked in a tobacco factory in Durham. My aunt had worked as a domestic for years in the North, had saved her money, and had then come to live with us. The only thing out of the ordinary about our life was the frequent and bitter quarreling between my father and Jesse, his older son.

But when I was fourteen, in 1947, my father died of cancer of the stomach; Aunt Jo had moved away, and she soon died of abdominal cancer; Jesse went into the Army, after threatening not to attend the funeral of his father—whom he now hated. (People talked, and he finally consented to attend.) Something destructive now entered that house in Wildwood. I was left dependent on my mother. I had been adored by my Aunt Jo, who used to catch me by myself sometimes and tell me what great things I was going to do in life—it was she who left me a legacy of six hundred dollars—but now there was only constant, intense criticism from my mother, who seemed to think that everything about me in every way was wrong.

Oddly enough the basic cause, the core of the hard knot of hostility against me, was the *book*. Once I had learned to decipher what was written on the printed page, that was literally all I wanted to do. I had learned how to walk inside a book, closing its cover behind me, and to stay there for long periods of time. It wasn't that I ignored the "real" world; it was simply that the *only* world that existed for me was the one I was in, inside the book. And, since the "real" world held so little for me, I escaped inside the book every chance I got. This caused problems.

When I was growing up I read from libraries, but after I started teaching, I liked to buy books. They cost money, and my mother regarded their purchase as a waste.

"Buying books all the time," she'd say. "You don't read them." This was another aspect of my reading habits that irritated her. I had learned to go into a book and quickly get from it the information that I wanted and discard the rest. But most galling of all to her was the obvious fact that I had no interest at all in housework. The curtains didn't interest me, neither did the slipcovers, and if the windows never got washed, I couldn't care less or even notice. Though I never *said* anything, my attitude must have shown, and as the years passed and my feelings were unchanging, my mother became more and more bitter.

"What's the matter with you, girl?" she'd say. "You're going to end up in Goldsboro." Goldsboro was the home of a state mental institution, and I was told many times that I was going to wind up there. And I halfway believed it, for I knew that I was different and felt that I was wrong, too. But nonetheless I persisted in my pattern of behavior, because it was the only one that made sense to me.

My mother always scolded in a very soft voice, never yelling, and since people in my culture yell and often "cuss" when they are mad, it was many years before I realized that these never-ending lectures by my mother were not reasonable lessons meant for my own good, but rather ways in which she could express some of the pain of her life—against a passive, unanswering target.

The weekend violence in the house next door, between my younger brother, Ruf Junior, and Louise, his wife, continued, and when it got so bad that I feared Louise was going to get seriously hurt, I called the police. Such incidents averaged once every three or four months. Although the violence stopped as the result of my calling in the police, both Nonnie, my mother, and Louise, the victim, acted as if I were in the wrong for doing so.

I don't know whether it was the fact that I would on occasion call in authorities or whether there was some other reason, but Ruf Junior continued to spread false rumors that I was a Lesbian, although he did not use high-class words like that. I think that that was probably why the rumor grew and became so tenacious. If one's own brother is telling it, a close member of the family, it will be more readily believed. Whatever the reason, the effect on my life was devastating.

Many times people would stop talking and stare silently as I approached, only to fall to murmuring among themselves as I passed by. What seemed to bother my tormentors the most was that occasionally my academic achievements brought me some small recognition or got my name in the Durham papers. They were secure in the knowledge that no one would come to the defense of an alleged "sexual deviate" or condemn them for the way they were treating me, and they were resentful because I was considered gifted. They were right. Nobody came to my defense; I learned over the years to endure in silence, hoping for the day I would be released from them.

One cold day my niece, Diane, was playing with "the boys," her younger cousins, Gerald and Arnold. They were chasing each other through my room and across the back porch, out the door, around the yard, then through the front door again in some enthralling game they had made up. On one trip through my room Diane lost her balance and fell against the wood-burning stove. A normal child would have recoiled instantly, but Diane leaned against the stove too long. When the pain finally reached her, she pulled away, leaving some of the flesh of her arm. I saw her looking at a raw red wound, and then her eyes met mine; there was such a terrible pain in them, for her own flesh was burning and she hadn't known it. She was different. I reached out and grabbed her to me, but she would let me hold her for only a few seconds. Then she joined the boys. But the look I saw on her face that day would come back over and over as one incident after the other made her realize that she was different. A sort of wondering pain.

Then something happened to Diane. I don't know whether it was the nature of her handicap—she had cerebral palsy and was retarded—or the fact that when she started to school the "normal" children mocked her, or whether it was the insanity in our household—or whether it was all three causes, but as the sixties progressed Diane was given more and more to vio-

59

lent rages. I learned to duck flying objects. Soon every door in the house leaned, leaving a scraped place on the floor—the result of having been forcefully slammed too many times. Diane's thundering feet and hurtling body and shocking curses would rage through the house like a hurricane. Pictures on the wall always hung slightly askew. But when her rage subsided, Diane was a sweet girl.

In the summer of 1958 I enrolled in summer school at the University of North Carolina–Chapel Hill. It was my first time in an integrated settting, except for the few nights I had spent in a creative writing class at Columbia University in New York City in the summer of 1956. What stands out most in my mind is that it was very hot that summer and I was very scared. I didn't know what I expected, but I was tense and nervous. I was even afraid to go into Lenior Hall for an occasional meal, though I was sure that that was where black students took their meals. Instead I drove on back to Wildwood.

But I enjoyed my classes—in English literature—and meeting and talking with people from different places. One of them was named Midori Sasaki.

An American literature minor, she was a lovely, fragile Japanese woman. We couldn't have been more unlike in appearance or temperament, yet she admired me, and when she made overtures of friendship I was, of course, startled, but I responded. I gave a dinner for her before she went back to Japan. We corresponded for several years and once, totally unexpectedly, a beautiful tea set, the kind that has cups without handles, arrived from Japan—a gift from Midori. It was just as lovely and delicate as she was.

At the end of summer I went back to Whitted Junior High, but I had subconsciously glimpsed the possibility of a new life. It would take another year or so to surface, though.

It was while I was working at Whitted that an incident happened that forever crystallized my relationship to black American males.

I needed a ride from Wildwood into Durham. Sammy, a college graduate, also worked in Durham. So I started riding with him. This arrangement lasted only two weeks. The first morning that I rode with him, Sammy talked on general subjects for a few minutes and then got to his main topic of conversation: *white women*, mainly the current crop of Miss America contestants. He discussed each one's attributes in loving detail with many whoops and hollers. His eyes gleamed, and he had a big smile on his face. I listened in stunned surprise but said nothing. Perhaps, I thought, he liked to discuss what was on TV, and when the pageant was over, the subject would change. But I was wrong. This topic was discussed every morning. When he had exhausted the current crop of Miss America contestants, he went back to the past and started discussing former contestants, one by one and in great detail. He was a smooth black, rather short and chunky, about thirty. As a younger man, he had worked in Canada for several summers; he had also been in the Army and thus considered himself something of a world traveler and sophisticate. Yet he seemed totally oblivious of the implications of his conversation on the self-esteem of black women, for he never held up a single black woman as attractive.

The end came one morning when the subject turned to Marilyn Monroe. She had visited American troops while he was stationed in Japan. He got started on her with the gleam and the big smile and the whoops and hollers. For some reason, I'll never know why, I got started on Marlon Brando and his good looks and obvious sexuality. So it was Marilyn/Marlon for a few minutes, until Sammy lapsed into total silence. I finished that week out, but he made an excuse and I had to find another way to go. Soon after this incident I bought a car and learned how to drive. I have often thought about that morning, but I have never been sorry that I responded the way I did.

There was a taboo against black males seeing white females in a sexual frame as well as a taboo against black females seeing white males in a sexual frame. Sammy felt, however, as did many black males of that time, that he could operate outside the taboo; yet he still tried to enforce it if it involved my commenting on white males. *I didn't see it that way.*

Light-skinned black women, incidentally, were often called "red-bones" by black males, less often "pinks," sometimes the grossly inelegant "yellowhammers," as in "I've got me a yellowhammer."

One day while I was seated hard by the A&P on Mangum Street near the hot-dog stand, I met myself. She was standing with a group of black women, all sturdy of figure and gleaming black in the sun. They had on their Sunday dresses but were not arrayed in their total paraphernalia, for they did not have on their Sunday shoes, nor did they wear hats. It was obvious that they had come in from the country to sell their tobacco, now that the Durham markets were open, and they wanted to dress better for the occasion than they did every day. So they wore the type of Sunday clothes sold by Raylass's, Freedman's, and the United Department Store: dark crepes with rhinestone buttons or with flounces that hung from the waist to mid-thigh. It was obvious by their expressions that they had made a sale, for they looked relaxed and smiling as they ate their hot dogs and drank big "drinks."

Suddenly, one of the women broke away from the group and started walking toward me. I didn't pay much attention to her; I thought that she wanted to get out of the hot sun and sit beside me on the bench. But it became obvious that she wanted to approach me about something. I was puzzled, for I did not know her, and she seemed rather timid about saying anything to me at all. Yet she stood there, finally saying hesitantly, "I hear that there's a tobacco factory where you can go through and see how cigarettes are made?" Her statement/ question was so unexpected that it took me by surprise, and I hesitated a moment before responding. Then I told her about the Liggett and Myers tour, on which I had once taken my eighth-grade class.

She brightened somewhat at this, but she still had another

question. "Can you go in the front door, just like everybody else?"

I wanted to cry at this point. But I responded, "Yes, you can go in the front door just like everybody else."

She thanked me and turned to join her companions standing in the sun, who couldn't care less about a factory tour and how the tobacco that they had spent many months working on was processed. Yet, one of them wanted to know. That was what made her different. She was me.

At a later time in my life I met another part of me. She was about thirty, of medium size, very dark, with shoulder-length hair which she wore in a pageboy. A neighbor who belonged to Reverend Sanders's church in Durham invited her to spend a week with him and his wife in Wildwood; she was a member of his church. He told me that she was a poet, and that she mostly kept to herself—and invited me to come over and talk with her.

I found her very difficult to talk to. She spoke slowly and sometimes seemed unwilling to respond at all, as if she did not trust me. But she showed me a book of her poems. It had been printed locally, on thick, glossy paper. A quick glance through it revealed that she used the hymn stanza and concentrated heavily on religious subjects. I admired her. With little means—she was not a professional—and, evidently, with little encouragement, she had written and published a book of her work. I never saw the poet again, and I don't remember her name

That fall I was dog-tired. Another school term had begun at Whitted, and it promised to be just like the old ones: discipline problems and more discipline problems. I was teaching little and felt that the students were learning even less. One of my colleagues called Whitted "Hell's Half Acre," and I had to agree that she was right. I had tried hard to heed the voices that told me what a good job I had in the Durham city school system, that many people had tried to get on and had not been able to. I tried to listen and be satisfied, for God knows it was better to be in Durham, close to familiar surroundings, than to be in the even more barren wasteland of eastern North Carolina, in Robersonville, or in Pinehurst, where black women were subjected to edicts from the police chief. But still I wanted better. I didn't know what would get me more of that indefinable something that I wanted, but I knew that I wasn't going to get it staying where I was.

One November day it rained buckets, and naturally the students couldn't go out at recess. The halls were crowded, the students restless. Discipline was impossible, so I gave up trying and stood and looked out the basement window of my classroom. Behind me there was chaos, bedlam, mayhem; outside the window I could see only the tires of passing cars. Above me, on the ceiling that I could practically touch if I stood on tiptoe, was the radiator. And there was no room anywhere, just for a moment, to be alone. While I was standing there a thought came to me so clearly that it was almost as if a voice had spoken out loud: *If you don't get out of here now, you never will.* And I moved with that voice. At the close of the school day I drove over to Chapel Hill in the rain to the University to apply for a National Defense Education Act loan.

When the receptionist directed me into the office, the loan officer, a tall, husky, red-haired man, rose from behind his desk to greet me. I was struck by this—and pleased. It was a good omen—the foreshadowing of the courteous treatment I would receive at the University of North Carolina.

4

In February 1960 I enrolled full-time at Chapel Hill. I had taken twelve hours there in the summer of 1958, so by the end of the summer of 1960 I would have completed the required course work for my master's degree and begun to write my thesis.

That decision on a rainy November day was one of the good

ones that I was sometimes able to make. Seldom have I been able to make good decisions, for I come from a culture that teaches that what is meant for you in this world you'll get, and what is not meant for you you'll not get. And not only that, but also it is prideful on your part to reach for something that you don't have. And you know what God does to those who are full of pride, don't you? He strikes them down.

At Chapel Hill my percentile score on the verbal part of the Graduate Record Examination was in the high 90s. In a course on the American novel that the chairman offered, the only undergraduate course that I had to take, I got an "A" on a grading scale that started at 96. No one at UNC called me in to question my high score. I could not help remembering that at the all-black North Carolina College at Durham, when I had scored high on some tests during my freshman year in 1951, I was questioned about it.

Instead, the chairman of the English Department at UNC, C. Hugh Holman, a Southern gentleman, always courteous and kind, became and remained my mentor throughout my course of graduate study. For the first time in my life my work was recognized, and I was given some support—this in an environment that I had been taught to suspect as totally and unrelentingly hostile and threatening.

One of the major problems faced by professional-class blacks in the 1960s in integrated situations, such as those at white Southern universities, was how to make it clear to the whites that there were significant differences of class and color among the blacks and that they, the whites, should observe them. The whites, however, refused to see differences, and the result was consternation and chagrin among those blacks who felt themselves to be of a higher status than the sons and daughters of the black folk who also attended the university.

Christa was one such black. A very light-skinned, attractive girl from Greensboro, she professed to have a great hatred for the University, where she was studying to get her master's degree. Every time I saw her, she would go into a diatribe against the whites at the University, and how glad she would be when she finished so that she could "get away from this place." I wondered about her vehemence, because she never recounted any specific incident in which she felt that whites had mistreated her, in class or on the campus. I had an idea about it, but I held my peace. The answer came one Sunday afternoon when a campus religious group gave an entertainment at which a singing group composed of some blacks from the town and one of the black maintenance men on the campus would perform. Christa and I were at the gathering. I didn't see Christa for a while; then she appeared, her face flaming.

"Do you know what that woman asked me?" she said.

I wanted to know, "What woman?"

It seems that the wife of a professor had incautiously asked Christa if she was one of the singers, and that had thrown Christa into a rage. I was rather amused, but I could see how perhaps for a student to be mistaken for a singer might be offensive to some. It wouldn't have been to me, but perhaps I am less sensitive about such matters than others are. Still I sensed an "X" factor in Christa's rage, but I held my peace. I wanted to be sure.

The answer came in the form of a student from northern Africa named Ihab. Ihab was the obsession of the black students. It was alleged that he went out of his way in a very ostentatious manner to avoid being anywhere near a black American. The blacks resented him bitterly because it was obvious that he had a large admixture of sub-Saharan black African blood. I wondered about this Ihab. Who was he?

Then one day I saw Ihab the Terrible—a thin, wiry man, who scampered down the high marble steps of the Louis Round Wilson Library. I laughed to myself. So this was the object of the black students' obsession. What did it matter whether he spoke or not? I couldn't care less. But a lot of blacks did. Without meaning to, Christa revealed why one day. She was commenting on his color (he was much darker than she) and his hair, which he wore very close-cut to conceal its Afro nature (hers was straight). Then she went over again the fact that he acted as if he abhorred black American students, ending her remarks with, "Even *me!*" I thought to myself, Why not you? But then I knew the answer. How he treated the dark blacks was Ihab's business, as far as Christa was concerned; but she was light-skinned, and he ought to see the difference. She hated him because he didn't. The year was 1960.

Other professional-class blacks used other techniques at UNC to point out their status to the whites. One woman from Durham, whose husband worked for a black insurance company, wore a large diamond ring; all during lectures she fingered it and caressed it and looked down at it. Surely a black who wore such an expensive ring deserved greater recognition from whites than one whose mother worked in a tobacco factory.

Then there was a man from Wilmington, a Johnny Mathis lookalike, who, whenever he could, started his class response with, "I play tennis and . . ." He felt that to play a status sport like tennis would surely point out differences between him and other blacks.

This "problem" among professional-class blacks lasted all during the sixties. To my knowledge it was never resolved.

Class and color conflict underlay much of the tension between black Americans and black Africans at the University. For example, there was the case of Alfred and Anna. Alfred was a handsome, witty young man from East Africa. He had an interest in writing and while he was at the University published a story in a collection that was edited on campus. Anna was from Mississippi. Skinny and short-haired, she looked like a typical soul sister. What worried the black Americans, both male and female, was that Alfred liked Anna and courted her quite assiduously. Their courtship was the subject of many a discussion in Lenoir Hall. *What does he see on her?* The American males resented the fact that she preferred a black African to them. Light-skinned black women also resented the fact that Alfred preferred Anna to *them.* Thus the talk went on. Finally, it was decided that he probably liked her because she reminded him of "the girls back home." This smiling comment became something of a standard joke in Lenoir Hall. Yet, an undertone of resentment always edged this remark. Later Alfred and Anna married and went to England, where he finished his education.

I had learned about Existentialism that year and decided to do my master's thesis with it as the basis: "Existential Themes in Ellison's *Invisible Man* and Wright's *The Outsider*" was the title. I spent hours and hours in the stacks of the Louis Round Wilson Library. It was exciting to learn about something that I didn't know about. Now the future looked brighter. When at last I received my M.A., I thought that I, too, would soon find my place as a respected scholar. (Fate, I now realize, was laughing gently at me.)

Part
TWO

5

A professor had taken a one-year leave of absence from the Department of English at North Carolina College at Durham, and I was given a temporary appointment as his replacement. The black folk in Durham felt bitter that the professors and administrators at NCC, a black college, considered themselves the *crème de la crème*, and indeed the college gloried in and promoted that image. Now I, an offspring of the black peasant-worker class of the rural South, would be in a position to observe those fabled "society" blacks up close. It was indeed a revelation.

So I returned to North Carolina College in the fall of 1960, this time as a faculty member. I dreamed of making my mark as a teacher and scholar, but things didn't turn out quite that way. The chairman of my department saw to that. Carroll Light, heavier and older, had just become chairman. Light had taught me English at the college.

The former chairman, who had made a rather tumultuous exit, remained on the staff. This created some problems for Light. So, in casting around for some way to firm up his position, Light struck on a tried-and-true formula: a research project. To help with his labors, he chose the newest additions to the faculty, Ellen and me. Ellen was a white member of the staff, and I had just escaped from the public schools of Durham and was very glad of it. I considered it an honor that I had been selected, and thought that things boded well for me in what had until now been the land of the enemy. I was rather ashamed of myself for the unpleasant memories I had of Carroll Light: his humorous approach to a paper I had written about some inner-city girls, and his air of incredulity at my graduation. I had just been too sensitive, I reassured myself. Now things were going to be different. I would work hard on this project and do a real bang-up job. Then, perhaps, the project would be published, and I would have my name on a piece of research. I had learned at UNC the importance of research and publishing. Now I had a chance to do both.

When meetings on the project first began, Carroll Light came. At these meetings there were also the director of research and development, Ellen, and I. But when the work started and each of us was expected to provide some input, often there were present at the meetings only the director, Ellen, and I, for Light usually had other business to attend to. The director provided what assistance he could, but this was not his project; he had other projects to supervise as well.

As the semester went on, Light's appearances at meetings became less and less frequent; then eventually they stopped altogether. There was nothing to do but abandon the project, for his role was a necessary one. Though he spoke airily of his duties and of the next semester, I felt that there was not going to be a next semester for this project, and I despaired. The time spent on it didn't bother me so much as the knowledge that it would never be completed.

My disappointment must have showed, for Light became unpleasant to me. But he did it in a strange way. He was never cold. On the contrary, he was hearty—jovial, even—but what seemed to me to be cutting remarks came thick and fast from him, always followed by a humorous comment, so that sometimes I wondered if I was hearing right. Was he deliberately insulting me, or was he making a joke? I could take a joke; the black folk from whom I came had used joking as one means of survival. But this sounded like something more.

Then there was the matter of his sitting down talking up to me without asking me to have a seat. Was that a personal peculiarity, or was he deliberately refusing to acknowledge that I had rights as a woman? I was deeply hurt by it.

I could see us together as we would have looked to any observer—the man confident and contemptuous, the woman bewildered and pleading. He a full-blown yellow man; she a tall, stocky, peasant-type dark-skinned woman. In that picture is the whole story of what segregation had done to an ethnic group. It had put one segment of it in control of the only means of amelioration of life for the whole group—education—and that segment determined who would get an education and on what terms; they also controlled who would work in the educational apparatus. It was not until the seventies, when the black shock troops of the sixties arrived on the campus as teachers and staff members—the black men and women who had spent the decade in faded jeans and tennis shoes and Afros, first struggling in the streets with the segregationists, then struggling on the black college campuses with the class racists—that some changes took place at colleges like NCC.

Harriet Williams, a fellow teacher, was about fifty-five years old, a little yellow lady with sparse hair and a heart-shaped face that she turned to the side when she smiled, just as did the early movie queens, from whom she had probably learned the gesture. The gesture seemed incongruous coming from someone with iron-gray hair and double folds over her eyes, but she had probably used it so long that now it seemed like second nature.

She stood around my office, telling me that she had heard about my good record and asking me what courses I had taken at the University. I mentioned some, and she perked up at the mention of Milton. She wanted me to understand that he was a favorite of hers. I wondered at the phrase "favorite of mine," but I let that go. Had I written a paper in the course? she wanted to know. When I said yes, she said she would like to see it sometime, for she had done some work on Milton herself at N.Y.U., and perhaps we could compare notes. Her comments were accompanied by a million head-on-the-side smiles. I was rather flattered that she had asked to see one of my papers, but explained that I had taken the course sometime earlier and doubted if I could find the paper now. But she persisted, saying that perhaps if I looked *real* hard I could find it, for she *so* much wanted to see it. I smiled and said that I would look at home. Harriet looked pixyishly up at me and went on. A pleasant lady, I thought.

Smiles deceived me for many years, long past the time when they should have. I mistakenly developed the notion that a friendly manner denoted real friendship.

It took some doing, but I found my paper on Milton. I showed the paper to Harriet the next day and she asked me to let her borrow it, suggesting that I stop by her house to get it later.

Harriet lived in a large, old-fashioned, two-story house, set a respectable distance back from the street in what used to be the most fashionable black neighborhood in Durham. It was such no longer, for the most expensive houses are now located about ten miles farther south, out in the woods. But evidently the house was built during the time when it was a sign of status to live in town, leaving the country, woods, and farmland to the black folk.

The lawn was neatly kept; the grass was always cut, which distinguished it from the surrounding area. Across the street was an empty, unkempt lot with a billboard, its message nearly peeled away, and less than a block away was a congested piece of real estate containing a hamburger stand and a juke joint. I have heard about the incongruous contrasts in neighborhoods in Latin America, particularly Mexico, where spacious houses and the rickety shanties stand in close proximity, and I imagine that such neighborhoods must be similar to black neighborhoods in the South built before vigorous zoning regulations were established, when people built "catch as catch can."

When Harriet opened the door, I got the impression of vast and dim space—something like a mausoleum. She led me across a runner to a chair—I was careful not to step onto the polished hardwood floor.

Harriet curled up kitten fashion in a wingback chair and smiled girlishly. I had a curious double vision: superimposed on the fiftyish face was that of a little girl with ringlets and bangs, in her best party dress and Mary Jane shoes, looking up for admiring adults to pat her on the head and murmur, "What a cute little girl you are!"

All was orderly in her home. The maid, a very black lady, sturdy and stolid, moved around quietly, bringing lemonade with cherries frozen in the ice cubes. I was really impressed by that little touch. Harriet seemed all set for gracious living. Heavy, sedate furniture was carefully arranged in fixed positions, and long draperies and filmy curtains flowed from fixtures on the high windows. Her husband, a retired businessman, she informed me, was upstairs resting. I had heard that he was very sickly when she married him.

We talked of this and that. Still I wondered uneasily about being there. Why? I felt guilty for being so suspicious. Finally, I asked her if she had read my paper.

Yes, she had read it. But it wasn't quite what she had expected, she said. I felt like apologizing for disappointing her. I didn't have nearly enough footnotes, she chided me, and footnotes were the very *essence* of scholarship. This timely truth was punctuated by a little girl's laugh. Why, when she was at N.Y.U. and wrote a paper, her footnotes took up over half of each page! I wondered why Harriet hadn't gotten her master's degree at N.Y.U., but she, like ninety percent of the faculty in the department, had gotten her master's, the highest degree she held, from a black college. In fact, a number of the staff members had gotten their master's from North Carolina College itself, the same one at which they were teaching. It was not until the late sixties and early seventies, when there was a glut on the Ph.D. market in the United States (one result of which was a flood onto black campuses of white Ph.D. holders desperately in need of jobs) that black faculty started seeking Ph.D. degrees in earnest. For the appearance of white faculty on the black campus caused consternation bordering on panic: up until the late sixties a master's degree was thought to be sufficient at a black college, leaving the doctorate to the chairman—who served for life! Occasionally one other male in the department or at most two might hold more advanced degrees. Everybody was happy with this arrangement: the staff didn't have to work seriously beyond the master's degree, and the chairman was assured that there were no challengers to the throne.

I tried to explain to Harriet that some professors at the university were then stressing the need for original insights into literature, and backing away from papers that were merely extensive compilations of secondary scholarship. But Harriet hadn't heard of such a trend. In fact, she wasn't interested in my paper, period. I had the feeling that she hadn't really read it, for she never commented on the content.

I was so hurt at the trick that I couldn't say anything. It was the first of a series of encounters with descendants of the mulatto class I was to have over the years, in which the underlying theme was, "You have been evaluated much too highly. Your rightful place is under us." And I would look right back at them, in a way that said, "You are as much an outsider from the dominant society as I am, so as far as I am concerned, unless you have done something to distinguish yourself, you and your opinion mean nothing to me."

I realize that the fact that I had performed competently at the University had caused hostile feelings to flare up in Harriet. The University was the enemy. By opening its doors to all blacks, and not limiting its admissions to blacks of a certain class or color, it had unwittingly removed the keystone that was holding black "society" together. For if the underclass of

blacks could move, ever so slightly, out from under, the mulatto class structure on top of them would crack and fall right
in. Integration gave the black folk another possible route, a
larger stage to play on. When the first member of the black
working poor set foot on the first Southern white campus in
the fifties and sixties, it was the beginning of the decline of
people like Harriet Williams.

Harriet followed me to the door, still cooing and kittenish.
In the hall on the piano was a garish statue of a man painted
jet-black, with no attempt made to duplicate skin tones. He
wore a long white chalky-looking robe. I recognized the sculp-
ture as Saint Martin de Porres, from a recent magazine article
about his canonization. I was surprised to see that jet-black
statue in her house. But he was a foreigner, so that explained
it.

I sometimes wonder even now about the society that produced a woman like Harriet. It was lacking in compassion and
plain civility. Those who tried to join it had to develop those
qualities of mind. In many small places and somewhat larger
towns that I lived in I observed people who felt that, since
there was no way out, they might as well be a part of whatever there was in the black world. What happened to them as
people was terrible to see.

The 1960s was no ordinary decade in the South, for it was
the decade that saw the end of a way of life—legal segregation
of the races—and the start of something that had never been
tried before. Customs would fade, institutions would crack;
some would fall and crumble completely, while others would
adjust. But none of them would be the same. No one knew *that*
in the early sixties, except, maybe, the whites. The blacks
thought that with the coming of integration the whites would
be discomfited, that the whites' world would crack. It never,
ever occurred to the black professional class that the black
world would undergo such changes that by the end of the
decade it would no longer resemble what it had been since

the beginning of the century. One of the ironies of life in the South is the fact that the black professional class, thinking that under integration it would entrench its position vis-à-vis black folk, instead found itself in many cases as discomfited by the changes as the whites were. As for the black folk, they could not have cared less; any change at all was a decided improvement for them.

Sylvia was a small-town girl, a country girl really, who moved to Durham and married. She had a house and a little boy, and was a librarian. Her husband was an accountant. What more could any woman ask? But the first time I met her I sensed her discontent, her lack of satisfaction. Sylvia was not in paradise; she had been unable to penetrate Durham's black "society." She moved on the fringe, but never could seem to get closer. The longer I knew Sylvia, the more puzzled I was by her attitude toward Durham's black "society." Did she really consider herself one of them, accepting their smiling put-downs, feeling that the periphery of that world was better than anything in the world of the black folk in that country town from whence she came? Or did she secretly resent them, but hate to admit that the price she had paid for the position she had attained hadn't been worth it? Even more chilling to me was the thought that Sylvia didn't know that she was not a member in good standing of Durham's black "society"; that when she thought that she was moving up, she was really still on the periphery, but because she was in motion she never knew the difference.

I think it was the fact that I had studied at the University that first drew me into Sylvia's ken. She would occasionally accost me when our paths happened to cross. On such occasions Sylvia had a peculiar stance. She was rather heavy, with something of a pouter-pigeon look. She would stand with one leg forward, the other one slightly back, both legs bent. This would throw her body out of kilter, so that she thrust her chest forward while she threw her head back. She would smile a big smile, warm and welcoming, but her eyes were without lights. That was the characteristic of her face that puzzled me most. I wondered what could have happened to a woman in her early thirties to cause her eyes to burn out like that. Her stance, which essentially was a coming-and-going one, was also curious. It was as if I both attracted and repelled her at the same time. She wanted to come toward me; she wanted to back away from me; and her body stayed off balance because she was never able to resolve that ambivalence. Her ambivalence was expressed also, I felt, in a characteristic gesture that she used. She raised her right arm chest-high, as if to protect herself from attack, at the same time leaving it in a position to chop out suddenly at me.

If Sylvia's eyes were strange, her skin was even stranger, for it had no color; it looked lifeless. I wondered about that for a while, until one day it came to me what the matter was. I had noticed that the skin around her eyes always looked darker than the rest of her face. Then I took note of her neck, arms, and hands, and, finally, I was sure. Sylvia had at some time in her life used a cream that had leached all the color out of her skin, taking with it the skin's natural elasticity and vibrancy. That was another price that Sylvia had paid; perhaps at that time she thought it was not too high.

At first when she would see me, Sylvia would merely exclaim, "Girl . . ." and pass along what she called little tidbits of gossip. Once she invited me to stop by her home. I was surprised to find that it was a conventional house—red brick, with the usual number of rooms. It was set back from the street in what could only be described as a congested neighborhood, with many commercial properties close by. I wondered at the location, but then decided that perhaps it was the reality of means conflicting with the illusion of aspiration that accounted for her living there. I sensed that Sylvia was calling me in as if to say, Look. See what I've got: the best that there is in black life. Who are you to reject it? It's better than anything you've got or are going to get. Stop struggling and try to find your place in the black world as it is, *for this is all there is.*

I never could see it that way. Now I realize that this feeling on my part underlay some of the tension and hostility that Sylvia exhibited toward me. On the one hand, she wanted to pull me close so that she could show me what she had; on the other hand, she wanted to push me away because I represented what she was trying to escape from, the black folk.

Sylvia called her son, Reginald Junior, a husky-looking child, and had him demonstrate his precociousness by sending him to the record bin to pick out his favorite record album— *The Music Man*! She was quite pleased at his accomplishment and turned to me to see what effect it had. I said something vague, like, "That is really something, isn't it?" But in fact was not impressed to see a black child admiring *The Music Man*. It wasn't classical music and it wasn't black music; it was strictly Middle America.

"Do you know Charles Randolph?" Sylvia asked. "You know, the musician?"

"Yes," I said.

Sylvia always assumed that I knew nothing of Durham, forgetting that though I lived in the country I naturally would have relatives and other contacts in the town. "Well, there is a man who comes to see him. He drives a white Pontiac, and he parks it right beside Mr. Randolph's big car." I knew what was coming next, for not only was Mr. Randolph a talented musician, he also was reputed to be homosexual.

"They say they're going together, and I believe it, because one day I watched. That car came there early in the morning and all that day I went back and forth, and every time I looked out it was still parked there. It was still parked there late that night. Neither car moved all day. Those two men had been in there together all that time. *By themselves*."

There wasn't much I could say. I could have pointed out to her the thought that crossed my mind, that neither she nor anyone else knew who was in Mr. Randolph's place and what went on there. But I said nothing, for I was listening to the way Sylvia was talking. She was highly animated—the lights had come on in her eyes, and her cheeks seemed flushed—and she was clearly enjoying the story she was telling. You might have thought that anyone as super-super-conventional as Sylvia would have shied away from such a story, but she was like a lot of prim and proper black professional women whom I have run into over the years; the more limited, restricted, and restrained their lives, the more interest and joy they take in talking about sex, certainly when it concerns someone else.

"Isn't this a disgrace?" she continued.

I murmured something.

"Child, I hear there's a whole ring of them."

Sylvia had forgotten herself when she reverted to the black folk expression "Child," which was something she rarely did, preferring to talk in what I at one time heard her refer to as a "nice" voice. Her concept of what was "nice" led her to pronounce "says" to rhyme with "pays."

"Do you know Richard Love?" she asked. "You know, he's one of the best students at the college, I hear."

"Yes, I know him." I didn't tell her that I had taught Richard Love in the eighth grade, where I remembered him as an extremely bright, personable boy. He was also very handsome: tall, slim, with smooth chocolate skin and black, black curly hair. A slightly crooked smile, probably a result of sucking his thumb as a child, was the only one thing that kept his face from a kind of classic beauty.

"Well, they say he's part of the ring," Sylvia said. "They say he's a prostitute. You know, he wants to go to school so bad and he doesn't have any money, so he goes out with them to get the money to stay in school. One night someone passed a car parked in the dark in back of the dormitory, and Richard Love was in it with one of them."

Sylvia paused, looking not at me but straight ahead, and I realized that she wasn't actually talking to me, but rather had gotten so engrossed in her own story and the hidden needs it fulfilled that for the moment I had been forgotten. I had served merely as an excuse for her to rehearse what she must have gone over in her mind many, many times. I was appalled at the casual viciousness with which she had destroyed Richard Love—for no reason at all, apparently, except that it made a good story. I wanted to say something, but I didn't; I had been an outsider so long and there had been so many complaints about my "attitude" that I had ceased to engage in interchanges with anyone, substituting a smile instead. I had to smile. It masked a lot of what I was thinking. For what I saw was a country girl who had lost much, but just how much I was yet to find out.

Though I invited her to my home, Sylvia would never come, making excuses about being unable to "go way out there." But I continued to visit her occasionally. It was on one such visit that I got the first hint of trouble in paradise. It was right after church on a Sunday. Reginald Senior, whom I seldom saw, was at home, dressed in a brown suit, with vest and white shirt. Reginald Junior was still in his church clothes too, but Sylvia had changed into a more casual dress, a muted shirtwaist, with pearl buttons halfway down and pleats all around. Trouble arose when Reginald Senior told the boy to go out on the lawn and get the paper. The grass was deep and uncut near the road. The boy objected. He didn't want to go.

His father said, "I said go get the paper, Reginald." The boy hung back, looking at his mother, waiting for her to say something. Sylvia got up and said, "That's all right, Reginald Junior. I'll go get it."

And at that moment I saw a flash of cold fury on the father's face. He turned to me, sort of as a mediator. "I don't want my boy to grow up to be a sissy," he said. "I want him to be an all-around boy. Able to get along with anybody. Able to talk with anybody. Not having just special people that he can talk to." Then he turned to the boy again, his voice measured. "I said go get the paper, and I mean go get it now."

"Reginald, you know he's been sick this week," Sylvia said. "He's not feeling well."

The father by this time was furious. "He's not too sick or too good to walk out there on that lawn and get the paper, and he's going to. And I mean right now."

By then both parents were standing facing each other in the doorway. The boy eased out between them and headed across

82

the porch. The father was standing, making sure that he went. The mother was standing as if waiting to protect him should something happen to him on his journey across the lawn.

The son came back, having safely negotiated the distance across the lawn and back and gave his father the paper.

The black professional mother who tries, perhaps too hard, to protect her son from some of the brutality of black life is an authentic type. Sometimes the results are disastrous.

Algernon, a big, banana-colored boy, was reputed to be one of the most brilliant students ever to graduate from the Durham city schools. He went off to an extremely prestigious Ivy League school, trailing the applause of Durham's black professional class. The trouble was that after arriving on campus he fell in with a group of homosexual young men whose activities were such that when the administration learned of them, they suspended the young men. Algernon came home. Keeping a low profile, he went out only at night, heavily muffled and with dark glasses on. He was readmitted, but his health had been shattered, and the next time he arrived in Durham, he was in his coffin. No one ever said how he had died. In conversation with me, his mother once alluded to what had happened to her son. She felt that the fact that he hadn't been raised on a farm and seen animal life, mating and so forth— "nature," she called it—caused the problems her son, a precocious and sheltered young man, had had.

Another such case concerned Dorothy, an extremely domineering and controlling woman—she was a teacher—who reared a son in such a fashion that his homosexual exploits were the talk of campuses in several Southeastern states. When, during the halcyon days of affirmative action, he was placed in an extremely high position as a civilian with the military, everybody was stunned.

One summer weekend as the days grew longer and hotter and time seemed to stand still, I went to New York City. I caught the eleven p.m. bus on Friday night, slept in a hotel for a few hours Saturday morning, got up and went to a matinee, looked around the city, and came home Sunday. I had done it several times before; even when I was teaching the eighth grade in Durham I periodically went to New York for a weekend and tried to see a play and visit at least one museum. I think that, too, was a part of my subconscious striving to form a new pattern, a new life-style.

On the following Monday afternoon I saw Sylvia, and somewhere in the conversation I started off a sentence with, "While I was in New York . . ." Sylvia burst out with "Not again!" It was as though the words were torn from her before she could catch herself. She was stunned that they had come out—pure feeling, so different from the mannered way in which she always spoke. I was equally stunned.

It couldn't have been envy of my going on a bus trip that had caused the outburst, for Sylvia had told me that summer of her trip with Reginald to the Playboy Club in Baltimore and how fabulously their friends there had entertained them. On another occasion, she had spoken of the Copacabaña in New York City and how her family had enjoyed themselves there. Those were places I hadn't been to, and perhaps would never go to. I had listened with interest, for I always wondered about different ways of living and doing things. Also I had once been treated to a slide lecture by Sylvia on "My Trip to Europe."

So a simple bus ride to New York City couldn't have been unusual for her. But I suspected that Sylvia envied my freedom. I was a total outsider, unfettered by anybody's rules but my own. The black working poor, the peasants, did not have a very wide view of the world, and though this wasn't their fault, their narrow views kept them tied in place, where one generation slowly walked around the circle until it closed, and following in its footsteps was another generation, and just behind them another generation, and it would go on forever, with the rut getting deeper but the path not getting any wider. The only way for the path to get wider was for someone to step outside the circle.

So I went to New York City; I went to the plays, I read the magazines, hoping that it would not be all in vain, that some-day the world would open up and have a place in it for me. I didn't have Sylvia's alternative. I was very dark-skinned. Bleach couldn't help that. Perhaps, if I could have, I would have played their game. But life had dealt me a different hand and I played it the best I could. I had spent a long time longing for a different hand. I made bargains with myself, with God, with Fate. "If only I had ..." Nothing, absolutely nothing, happened. When all the prayer and the pleading had stopped, I was still holding my original hand. So I stopped looking for another hand; the choice was mine. I could either build a dif-ferent life for myself, or I could lie down and die.

I saw no reason why Sylvia couldn't live a freer life, until, quite unexpectedly, the answer came.

Without calling first, in fact without even thinking about it, I stopped by Sylvia's house.

There were no other cars there, so I didn't expect her to have company. But she did. There was a plump, brown lady sitting there, her face moist in the heat, though the house was air-conditioned. I thought that Sylvia had got a new maid. Sylvia made no effort to introduce us, while I explained to her that if she wasn't using her electric frying pan, I would like to borrow it overnight and would return it on Sunday. Sylvia said, "Of course," and disappeared into the back to get it.

I stood waiting for Sylvia to come back. Then the lady said, "You look just like my cousin." I smiled at her, recognizing the conversational ploy often employed by black folk when they want to show themselves friendly in a new situation. They tell you that you remind them of an aunt, mother, sister, uncle, brother, father, whoever. It is meant as a compliment. Then you say, "Sure enough," and they say, "He's about your height," or your complexion, or they point out some other particular that reminds them of the relative. That done, the conversation proceeds to something else.

I said, "Where does she live?" Also a standard ploy. It gives the other speaker a chance to tell you something about himself, herself, where his home is, or the relatives he has in New York City.

The lady mentioned a nearby farming community, and I knew who she was. Just then Sylvia came back with the pan and found us chatting amiably. That was when she said, in an offhanded sort of way, "This is my mother. She's come up to visit me for the day."

I had never seen Sylvia's mother and had rarely heard Sylvia refer to her, as she never referred to her folks. Now I knew why. One of the prices Sylvia had paid in trying to penetrate black "society" in Durham was the near total erasure of her past, for none of it fitted the new identity that she wanted to assume. Her mother, sitting there in her wilted cotton dress, was the quintessential black worker, either on the farm or, as I suspected, as a domestic for some of the local whites in Sylvia's hometown. I stood looking at the smiling lady, sitting with her plump hands face up in her lap, her plump legs crossed at the ankle; to me she looked like the one million "Sisters" in the Amen corners of black Baptist and Methodist churches every Sunday morning in every black community in the nation. They are the missionary ladies: some go to see the sick; others sing in the choir; they serve as flower ladies when members of the church die. They work hard for a living, have little education and even less sophistication. And they are the backbone of the American black ethnic group.

Sylvia looked a little chagrined and plainly wanted me to go. So I said good-bye and left.

I could have been triumphant after I saw Sylvia's mother, but instead I felt a kind of horrified pity for what she had done. I didn't feel gleeful, because I knew why she had done it. I knew the reason for the affected language, the stilted manner, and the "nice" voice; I knew the reason for the bleach. I could see her as a young girl, growing up a black in a farm community in North Carolina, ambitious, but with no way out. She was light-brown-skinned but not *light enough*, and she knew that that shade of difference was the difference between a higher status and a lower one in the black world. So she bought some salve from the Lucky Heart man and started using it on her skin, hoping for a lighter tone, just one tone lighter. Then she worked on her language, carefully constructing sentences like those in the novels she read; not earthy, realistic novels, but novels about highborn ladies or people of great prestige and wealth. If she had to forsake naturalness, that was just the price that she had to pay. She decided that she would go to college when she grew up and have a better life than those of the people she left behind.

Then she had to consider carefully the type of college that would help her with her plans. She wanted to marry, so she would go to a co-ed college, but she didn't want to marry a farm boy or craftsman, so that would eliminate A&T at Greensboro, the state's agricultural and technical school for blacks. She would go to college in Durham, for she had heard that "rich" blacks lived in the town, and there she might meet a son of a "rich" family and marry him and soon be in the social world, safe at last from the life in the farming community. She carefully eliminated those childhood friends who wouldn't fit into this image; she couldn't have them showing up in Durham, spoiling her new life.

When she got to Durham, she discreetly studied the social structure at North Carolina College, selecting those whose status was the highest, being "nice" but distant to those who weren't the proper sort. She further gained her way by being compliant and cheerful. Then she met Reginald. And though his family was only on the periphery of Durham society, it was close enough. So she was sweet and easy to get along with, and eventually she won him. He was ambitious and soon had his own small firm. Her future was assured. But something was missing. Her new life did not bring her the happiness she sought. She did not make a deep inroad into her new life. There was a hard core of Durham society that refused to acknowledge her existence. But still, to be on the periphery was better than nothing. And those people who weren't in were really nowhere at all.

Sylvia had made all of her basic life choices by the late forties. For the world at that time, her choice was a logical one, considering what she wanted out of life and her options. But the choice that she made was already obsolete, for in 1954, when the Supreme Court held that segregation in the public schools was unconstitutional, the world started to change.

Ida wanted to be a member in good standing in Durham's black professional class, just as Sylvia had; only she chose a different route. A dark-skinned, plain-looking girl with "stubbed" features and a gap between her front teeth, Ida followed the path sometimes taken by other women similarly situated: she decided to "hang around" with the highly prized light-skinned girls, feeling that some of their popularity would rub off on her and that she would get party invitations and, eventually, a husband. Their condescension toward her was not too high a price to pay for the privilege of being in their company and the opportunities that might come her way.

Her personal relationships with men were the same. A registered nurse, she met a teacher, "a pretty man"—that is, he had caramel-colored skin and a crispy type of hair that held oil well. Such men were highly prized. He rather tolerantly let her chase him for a number of years, occasionally bestowing his grace on her, until he found someone he really cared for; then he quit Ida.

Time brought integration in the schools. The ex-boyfriend wanted an administrative job, but he had a problem. The girl he lived with, whom he really loved, told their friends that he was not man enough for her, then handed their daughter over to him and left the state. His mother took the child and reared it. Now he was fearful of what his chances for advancement were if it became known that he had an illegitimate child. So he asked Ida, who was nearing forty, if she wanted to marry. *Did she want to marry?* Ida not only bought a long white satin gown and sent her picture in it to the morning paper, she also went to see people she hadn't visited in years, to smirk and tell them about the news.

So she had a church wedding, with her husband's daughter present, and accepted the task of rearing the other woman's child. People laughed about it, but Ida was glad to get a husband.

There was a black woman in Durham who did a thriving business in labels stolen from Ellis Stone, the Bergdorf's of Durham. Her customers were black public-school teachers who bought garments at Belk's, the Gimbels of Durham, but wanted their clothing to carry the labels of the more prestigious store.

Once I was seated in the Lincoln Hospital clinic waiting for one of Durham's black physicians when the telephone rang. It was located in the next room, hard by the door. A woman patient was calling to talk to him about her former physician, one of the early black practitioners in Durham. "My" physician promptly launched a sustained, vicious attack on the competence of this man. A few minutes after this conversation ended, the physician who had been the object of the attack called "my" physician, who promptly and vehemently denied saying those things to "that woman." Then he called "that woman" and in a cajoling conversation chided her for repeating what he had said.

All these conversations were held in a voice so loud that not only I, seated in the next room, but also anyone in the immediate vicinity could hear them.

Two public-school teachers, women, were "tight" friends. One was having marital problems so severe that she often summoned her friend in the middle of the night to counsel her and give her emotional support. Her friend always responded. Once, however, in an unguarded moment, the Good Samaritan confided to her "friend" that there was an irregularity in her teaching credentials. Her "friend" told the principal. The Good Samaritan lost her job and had a severe nervous breakdown.

A black worker at the tobacco factory at lunchtime changed into a suit, shirt, vest, tie. He carried a copy of *The Wall Street Journal* and made a careful tour of downtown Durham. He wanted to be taken for an executive of the black insurance company.

Black Durham "society" thrived on sex scandals among its members. A black physician decided to change wives. The woman of his choice was already married, but they solved that: they each left their respective mates and, while the divorces were pending, black Durham talked and talked. A few years later, after they were married, there was a shooting at their home, and he was hospitalized. Black Durham talked and talked and talked and talked.

A man with a longing to play a role in public life surprised his spouse in a motel room with another man—a teacher at the college—and black Durham talked and talked.

There was a woman, a schoolteacher from a prominent religious family, who went on paid assignations, partly from ego need and partly to help pay her bills. Black Durham talked.

During the early, heady days of integration, a black wife walked into the kitchen during a party at her house and found her college-teacher husband in an embrace with one of the white women guests. There was a scene. Black Durham talked.

The wife of a civil-rights leader and attorney found in her husband's car the checkbook of a young woman who was an employee of North Carolina Mutual, a large black insurance company. Talk.

A Durham schoolteacher paid a surprise visit to her husband, who was a graduate student at Howard. She found in his bed the daughter of an executive at the Mutual. Talk.

6

Ellen had thought of the idea of a club that would meet once a week so that majors in the department could talk on an informal basis with members of the faculty. It had met several times, but didn't seem to be generating much interest. Now she thought that perhaps a planned program at each meeting would draw more students, and so she asked me to be in charge of the program.

I had been stimulated by the programs that I had attended at the English Club when I was a student at the University in Chapel Hill, and wanted to plan something similar at the College.

At the University coffee had been served for about half an hour before the scheduled talk, during which time faculty and students in the department met and socialized. Afterward there was a question-and-answer period. So I adopted that format and set about trying to find speakers. I invited members of the department; two of them came, but the others backed off, as not having anything to talk about with the students. So I decided to use the resources of the community in the Durham–Chapel Hill area. There were many writers in the area, most of them attached to the large universities, and some of whom I had met.

I called one of the most successful writers and asked if he would be interested in coming to North Carolina College to talk to the club. I told him we had no money to pay him. He said, "It's right across town, and I'll be glad to come." I publicized it in the local paper, which drew some townspeople as well as students other than majors, and faculty members other than those in the department. There was a large turnout, and the meeting was a success. I was exhilarated. At last I was doing what I liked to do; I had found that the current of ideas that floated outside the formal classroom, particularly those emanating from people who passed through the University, were most helpful in enlarging my view of the world. A chance remark, an offhand comment, and something that hadn't been in my thinking at all would suddenly emerge.

Among the speakers who came was Paul Green, a white playwright who lived in Chapel Hill and once had been a collaborator of Richard Wright's. He related an incident involving Wright's stay in the town while they were working on a stage version of *Native Son*. Richard Wright roomed with a black family, and the two men used an office loaned to them by the University while they worked on the play. Somehow word got out that there was a black man on the campus at the University, that he was a Communist, and that his wife was white. Some of the white locals, already hostile to the University and to Paul Green, decided to make an example of Wright and plotted to do him harm. When someone told Green what was going on, he went into town to Eubanks, the drugstore where the locals "hung out," and started talking with them. They were angry; if Wright didn't leave, something bad was going to happen to him. Since Green knew one of the men very well—he was a cousin—he attempted to reason with him, but the man was adamant. They were going to move against Richard Wright that night.

There was a field of tall grass in front of the home where Wright was staying, so Green went out in the field and stayed there all night, so that if the gang came he would be in a position to be of some help. However, the gang never showed up, and Wright continued his work there in the town without incident, evidently without ever learning of the threats made against him.

Several months later, the scene of their collaboration shifted to New York City. Green was staying in a Manhattan hotel, and Wright came to see him there. On the second day that Wright came, the playwright got a call from the manager. "There's a colored fellow on the way up. He says that he's coming to see you. We let him come on up this time but we can't have this." When Wright got to the room, very angry and upset, he said, "This place is worse than Chapel Hill."

The speakers continued, including a lady who did dramatic scenes from Tennessee Williams's plays and a psychiatrist who had proved to his satisfaction that Hamlet's problem was that he was immature, an adolescent really. That provoked quite a bit of reaction from the audience. I was very happy that whole semester. I was doing something that I personally liked very much, that I thought was a worthwhile contribution, both to the student body and to the townspeople.

Later that spring I ran into the writer who had been our first speaker.

"Hey," he said, "I've got exciting news. Ralph Ellison's coming to a symposium at Duke in the fall. Isn't that great?"

I, too, was excited. "I wonder if he'll come over to the College, if we invite him," I said.

"He probably will," the writer said. I was genuinely elated. I had read *Invisible Man* as soon as it came out and was delighted to think that the author was going to be right there in Durham! I wondered how we could get him to come. But then it shouldn't be too hard, I thought; for Tom Flowers, who had recently joined our faculty, had told me on several occasions that he had once been a very good friend of Ellison, especially at the time he was writing the book.

So the next day I stopped by Tom Flowers's office.

"Great news," I said. "Ralph Ellison is coming to town in the fall. It's all set. He's going to be on a symposium at Duke. Perhaps, since he's right here in town, we can get him to come over. Since you know him, will you get in touch with him and ask him to come?"

Flowers didn't seem too excited about it. "I'll see what I can do," he said.

I felt a little put down by Flowers's reaction, but then, he was much more sophisticated than I was: big-city man, full professor, degree from a prestigious Northern university. I was still naïve enough to get excited about a writer.

Just before school was out for the summer I spoke to Flowers about the Ellison trip again and asked him if he had got in touch yet. He said he hadn't. I must have looked disappointed, for he asked me when he was supposed to come. I told him in October, and he said that there was plenty of time. On thinking about it, I realized that perhaps there was plenty of time. It was just that I had heard that sometimes speakers are booked months in advance, and I had thought that the prudent thing to do was to get in touch early.

A few days before school closed, Ellen told me that the president of the College had called her in for a conference. It seems that he had received many comments about the fine programs the English Club had been putting on, and he was distressed to learn that the club had no budget. How did the club get the speakers to come? When he heard that the speakers had come free of charge, the president suggested that the club submit a budget request, so that next year it could pay its speakers.

This was done, and the president wrote Ellen a letter telling her that the English Club had six hundred dollars for the next year. The president retired that year, and Ellen left to go back to graduate school, leaving the folder of club material with me. I became the head of the club.

When school started in September, I spoke to Tom Flowers again about Ellison, but he said that he'd wait until Ellison got to Durham, and perhaps something could be worked out then. I didn't know how things were done in the big time, but this didn't seem quite right to me. Still I waited, for I thought that Tom knew the way things were done; from the way he talked, he had lived in all the great cities, had known some of the important thinkers who lived in those places, and was, in general, from the big world out there. I felt that I had had little exposure, didn't know the correct way of doing things, and was afraid of trying to get in touch with Ellison myself.

Finally, realizing that nothing had been done or was going to be done, I called Mr. Ellison in New York. He told me his schedule and said that if it could be arranged, he'd be glad to come. That done, I told him our budget and asked him if he would come for half that sum. He agreed to. So we had a major speaker for three hundred dollars. It was a coup.

Ellison spent the better part of a day on our campus. He attended an autograph party in the afternoon, which had been given a notice in the newspaper, so some townspeople came. Then he gave a speech in the evening. The response was so great that many students sat in the aisles and stood at the back to hear him. He confessed himself to be "much moved." Then, after his speech and the long question-and-answer period, he came to a party that I gave at my apartment.

I had been rather shy about asking Ellison to come, because my apartment was practically bare. But when he accepted, I asked some friends to help. The chairman of the art department, a good-talking buddy, brought paintings and turned the walls into a miniature gallery. Two former neighbors came from Wildwood after they got off from work and arranged everything, then stayed through the evening, helping with the food preparation and serving. Some people whom I knew at the University brought flowers, food, and drink. The guest of honor proved to be an amiable raconteur. So the evening for me "ripened and fell open." When the last guest had gone and my friends had straightened up the apartment for me and gone back to the county, I fell asleep in a blissful state. It was the type of evening that I wanted to make a part of my life-style, indeed the only life-style that I really liked: to be around aware people, talking about interesting or amusing things. That night was a happy night for me and I slept soundly. I didn't know it then, but it was to be one of the few really happy occasions in my life for nearly seven years.

Several days later I got an angry letter from the new president of the College; he had taken an interest in the event and had given the club twenty-five dollars for refreshments himself. In the letter he said that he had been informed that the

English Club had no budget, that the English *Department* had funds for speakers, and he wanted me to explain things to him.

I was astounded. At first I didn't know how to respond. I wondered how the English Department could have a speakers' fund, when to my knowledge it never had sponsored a speaker of any sort. In my naïveté I spoke to the chairman, Carroll Light, about the letter, wondering how the new president could have been so misinformed; he had just assumed office and didn't know about the decisions that had been made the previous spring by his predecessor. The chairman looked blank and denied any knowledge of it. Fortunately, Ellen had kept a neat file of correspondence between herself and the former president regarding the matter of the English Club—how pleased he was that it had been a success and asking the club to submit a budget for next year. I took this correspondence to the new president; he read it and said that it was okay.

The president was satisfied, but still, I wondered who had misrepresented the facts to him in the first place and why. The answer was all around me, yet I didn't want to believe it. Finally I had to realize that some of the faculty had evidently been chagrined because a woman instructor in the department had put together a successful program, while they—of higher rank—had done nothing to promote Ellison's visit.

I had worked so hard and had surmounted so many obstacles in my quest for an education, the education that I believed would lead me to a better life. Yet it seemed to me that all my life I would have such people as these around me and would have no hope of somehow leaving a mark, some visible evidence that I, too, had once existed.

Depression became my closest companion. I learned it intimately. It was a gray, heavily laden cloud that gradually swung lower and lower, until it gently settled on me, pinning me down wherever I was, leaving me unable to move for days, then for weeks. Or depression was my walking along the edge of a cliff, when the grass was long and slippery. Depression was my foot slipping toward the edge. There was no help; once the slide began I knew that I would get to the edge and then go over. Sometimes, once I started down, I would deliberately push myself to the bottom. If I tried I could push myself to the bottom of a depression in one week. Then I would lie on the bottom, astounded, for about two weeks, then start back up again. But if I fought the depression off, once the slide began, I could hold on for six weeks before I hit the bottom; I had energy for nothing, however, except the fight. Gradually, bit by bit, I'd creep over the edge, catching any object in sight that would break my fall, but knowing all the time that I eventually was going to reach bottom before I could start up again.

Depression is a malady that I would not wish on my worst enemy.

It was also this experience that produced the first major break in the rather simplistic fundamentalist religion that was my heritage. An injustice had been done, but the people who had done it were not punished. No one rose up to champion my cause. Yet I had been taught that the right will prevail. But right wasn't prevailing. How was I to square that with my raising in the black Baptist church? The challenge to my beliefs so shook me that I took another tack. Perhaps in some way I had offended God and He was punishing me. Or perhaps He had some work for me in life and was testing me to make sure that I was strong and steadfast enough for the task. I tried hard to hold on to the latter beliefs, since I realize now that the first belief, that good doesn't automatically prevail, that people with power often abuse it if they are not challenged, was really my position all along. It was a long time before I could come to accept it.

I had first gone to a therapist in the spring of 1955, when I realized that, in spite of leading my class in this same college for twelve quarters and graduating *summa cum laude,* I would get no help from the Department of English, the College, or anyone else. I went to Duke Medical Center weekly for several months; my therapist was a Norwegian. When I felt better about life, I stopped going.

7

I was deep into my twenties and I wasn't married and the black folk wouldn't let up. "Are we going to eat cake this Christmas?" some would say in a joking manner, but they were not kidding. Others were more blunt: "When you going to get married? What are you waiting for?" And they weren't smiling either.

I was not alone in this. Once Marian told me about an incident that occurred when Ida saw her on the bus. They hadn't seen each other for a long time, but Ida jumped right in: "When you going to get married? When people get as old as you are and they're not married, people think there's something wrong with them." Marian was four years older than I. She was still steaming when she told me about it. Ida felt free to make such a remark although she was married to a man who (as they say) wouldn't work in a pie factory, and who promptly left her at each pregnancy and stayed away until the baby came. Still Ida felt that her state in life was the right one and anybody outside it was due for some serious questioning from the community.

Then I can remember Hazel's rage when she told me of a similar incident, in which Mamie questioned her about her lack of a boyfriend and wound up telling her, "The trouble with you and your friend Mary Mebane is that ya'll scared of men!" What both Mamie and Ida meant was sex. To the black folk that was nature, and anything not following what they considered nature's path was "unnatural." Shortly after Mamie made this observation, Hazel hurried up and found her somebody and married him.

But I was the holdout; and when they questioned me, I'd say, "Well, I don't know anyone." And they'd say, interpreting me correctly, "He doesn't have to be an educated man. There are plenty of men. Construction workers make good money, and bricklayers make a whole lot more than you do teaching." And I'd wring and twist and say something about being unattractive, but they'd come right back at me with Jane and Sally and Sue, who were plain-looking and married and had good husbands. Then I'd be silent, for I wouldn't tell them—and was ashamed to admit even to myself—that I wanted to marry a cultivated man, one who could appreciate me and encourage me. I felt that if I had some encouragement from those close to me, even just a little, I could do things that would make everyone proud of me, and would make me proud of me, too.

Then there was the fact that men didn't seem to like me, not even to talk with. I was always reading something and longing to talk about it with someone! So when I had a chance I would start talking to them about it, but the conversations ceased abruptly.

I would try to marry. I knew that it would be difficult, but I hoped not impossible. The attempt was the biggest mistake of my life, my descent into hell.

At that time in Durham there was a European lady, a wealthy widow, who spent her time proselytizing for the Baha'i faith. Her favorite method of recruitment was to give large parties, inviting the foreign student populations at Duke and Chapel Hill, along with some Durham people who were likely prospects. A colleague of mine at North Carolina College was a Baha'i and also an ardent proselytizer, so she invited me to one of the gatherings. It was held in October, on United Nations Day, and I was indeed surprised to see so many nationalities represented there. I enjoyed talking with the foreign students, and my hostess, evidently seeing my pleasure and thinking that perhaps I would make a good convert, called me several days later and invited me to dinner at her house.

Guests at the dinner were several white Americans, several black Americans, and several foreigners, one of whom was an African. I sat next to him, and he told me about his country in West Africa: the geography, the climate, the ways of the people. During the meal, when the hostess asked the African about his family, he said that his parents were dead and that he had been raised by relatives. She asked him specifically, right there in front of nine people, if he was married, and he said, "I am single." He was in the United States as a graduate student studying public health.

His first name was John. I was rather surprised at that, but he assured me that English first names were not uncommon in his country. In his country, he said, he had been a teacher and he had been trained in a school run by missionaries. John was far blacker than any American black I had ever seen, and he was dressed immaculately. His close-cropped hair was freshly barbered; his watch and his gold-rimmed glasses looked as though they had been polished forever; and his dark blue suit and black polished shoes gleamed, as did his stiffly starched white shirt. His manner was grave. He had the air of a man weighed down with heavy responsibilities, a person of whom much was expected.

I was immensely pleased to meet him, for it had long been a favorite theory of mine that black Africans were a noble people, far nobler than black Americans.

The next day John called me. He asked, in a rather formal way, how I was; then he mentioned some things from our conversation the previous evening, particularly some points about Africa that I had raised. I was flattered that he had called, and I responded warmly to him. He called the next day and the next. And soon he was calling morning and afternoon and in the evening also. I couldn't believe that there was someone who was really interested in me, but he seemed to be. His religious background was evident, for he often prefaced his statements with the phrase, "As our Lord says . . ." I had never heard that expression in ordinary conversation, so I figured that it must have been the English influence on his education that accounted for it.

In about a week, he said he would like to come to see me, but that he did not have a car. His budget was very limited, and he got around mostly on foot and on buses, for taxicabs were too expensive. I knew that the cost was prohibitive, for I was five miles from the center of town and nearly that distance again from the place where he was living. So after John had mentioned several times that he would like to see where I lived and meet my mother and so on, I invited him to Sunday dinner and said that I would come and get him.

He came. He amused my niece, Diane. He talked to my mother about religion, and that pleased her greatly. Everyone was quite happy that there was a man coming to see me at last. He stayed most of the afternoon, and then I drove him home. Home was for him a large old rooming house in Durham.

John's attentions increased. Some churches in Durham invited him to give slide lectures, often at the Sunday evening service. He would talk at great length about how much he looked forward to going, asking would I like to go, and if I said yes, he would say, "Well, come and get me." After a while he didn't have to say that, for on signal, I would tell him that I would come and get him. On these occasions he always wore African dress, with the long colorful cloth draped over an ordinary dark suit.

I don't know if he got paid for these appearances, for he never said anything. I doubt, however, that any church would have invited someone without tendering a fee, and a stranger from a foreign land probably would command an even higher one than a local speaker. But whether he got paid or not, he never offered me anything for the expense of the trip. Had he done so I would have refused it, but the fact that he didn't offer to do so seemed odd to me, and it stuck in my mind, however hard I tried to dismiss it as perhaps another custom of his country with which I was not familiar.

Soon John, in a passive sort of way, asked me to come to his room. I had many feelings of dread, for I feared human contacts in general and had felt even more threatened by the thought of physical contact. And then I feared God, for I had been taught this was against His teachings. Yet I had strong physical needs myself and greatly despaired at having been shut out of human life so long. Underlying the whole was the knowledge of what some people said behind my back about my lack of interest in men.

I thought about John's invitation for a long time and then decided to go. On the day before I was to visit him I woke up in the early morning to the sound of my heart beating. I was terrified, sure that I was about to have a heart attack. My heart was beating so loudly that the sound filled the room. I wondered why Diane, who slept in the next room, didn't wake up. I thought to myself that if I lay quietly for a while perhaps it would slow down, for I had never heard my own heartbeat before. I lay still, listening, waiting to see what would happen, but nothing did. I braced myself for the chest pains that I had read were signs of a heart attack, but I didn't feel any; my breathing didn't seem to be unusual either, just the loud sound of the beating of my heart.

The next day I got up and went to my classes, worried, not knowing what to do, hoping that the loud sound would go away, watching other people to see if they could hear it. But no one seemed to hear. Still I found it difficult to talk and to concentrate. Finally, in the afternoon, I realized that something was very wrong, and I went to the Emergency Room at Duke University Medical Center, explaining that for some reason my heart was beating so loudly that I could hardly hear anything else. The doctor listened to my heart, then while I was lying on my back he pressed very hard on a point between my throat and upper chest. The pressure gradually slowed down the beat of my heart. In about half an hour I could no longer hear the beating.

There was another reason why I was so nervous about going to a man's apartment, a reason that I didn't want to think about. Aside from any moral or ethical reasons, or even my own physical needs, there was the terror that I had experienced one summer night long ago, when I was five years old. That summer we were building a new house, and there were several men helping who were staying with us, sleeping in the barn because the old house was torn down. Late in the night I got up to go to the outdoor toilet. Somewhere out there in the stormy night something happened to me, something so bad that I had erased all memory of it. I think that someone grabbed me and hurt me in some way, but I could never be sure, for, try as hard as I could over the years, that was one memory that I could never recover.

But I overrode all doubts and fears that I had. My mind was made up. I would go.

A more inauspicious introduction to sex no one ever had. All I remember are fear and panic. First I eased quietly out of our house, after midnight. I left by the back door, but the car was parked in the front, so I doubt that my leaving was unheard or unobserved either by my mother or our neighbor across the street, who had odd sleeping hours.

In an effort not to attract attention, I held the car door open with my left hand while I backed up in the yard and rolled gently out of the driveway, slamming the door only as I accelerated a short distance up the road. I thought that I was on my way to happiness and a husband. In fact, the husband part came first, for I sincerely believed that only in marriage could one achieve happiness.

I knew it was a mistake the moment I arrived at the house where John was making his home. It was dark, but I could see the yard was bare, showing hard-packed earth, with grass in patches. All over the yard were the huge swollen veins of the exposed roots of trees. The house was poorly situated, at the bottom of an incline, down from the street, so that the porch was almost level with the ground. The two-story house looked unprepossessing, with peeling white paint and rusty screens.

This was definitely not my idea of a romantic setting. Class, style, and elegance mean a lot to me.

Somehow the pictures in my mind didn't jibe with the bare, hard-packed yard and the gnarled roots of trees, or the rusty-looking screens set amid the peeling paint. Our hurried whispered greeting on the porch—for his landlady lived on the first floor—and stealthy climb up the stairs were also disillusioning. But even then I could have overlooked the surroundings if the trip had been worth the effort.

To the stealth and furtiveness, both of which I hated, was added a crushingly disappointing experience. It took John a very long time to get an erection, and he could maintain it for one minute at most. It was awful, and I had no idea what to do or say. We lay in silence for a long while. Then I told him I had to get home, and he seemed rather relieved. I went home, devastated by disappointment and even more by John's insinuation that his failure was my fault, that my ignorance and lack of expertise had crippled him. In my naïveté I bought his thesis one hundred percent. Now I had another burden on me.

John's attentions continued, however, for several weeks. I continued to see him, for, though the physical debacle was crushing and his jeering at me was cruel, I considered him a very eligible man, particularly now that he had "known" me. So I subdued all doubts that surfaced in my mind and smiled to cover my disappointment, having experienced, to some extent, the one aspect of "life" that the folk seemed to think I had been missing.

But soon John cut his telephone calls to one per day, then to one every other day. When he let a week elapse, I became distraught; if a man who had "known" me didn't marry me, what was to become of me? In the eyes of the church I was a sinner and in the eyes of the community an outcast. I know now that these harsh judgments were mainly in my own mind.

Even more incredible now, from the standpoint of the

eighties, was the conviction I had, along with many contemporaries, that a physical encounter must result in either marriage or lifelong shame. Much of the rigidity of that position resulted from pressure on the black folk community by the white society surrounding it, constantly accusing it of wrongdoings. The "respectables" among the black folk responded with a sexual conservatism that can only be described as reactionary, but was made more palatable by being cloaked in the church's garments. The "nonrespectables" among the black folk didn't care, having the freedom to do as they pleased.

Not having heard from John, I called him. He didn't handle things very well: he was cold. Somewhere in the depths of my subconscious I knew that there was truth in a rumor I had heard; I said to him, "I know you're married and have been keeping it secret while you're here, and I'm going to tell it." Once I shouted it into the telephone, the effect on him was electric. He denied it and said good-bye. Then he called me every twenty minutes or so to deny it again—until I refused to pick up the telephone. When he did get through to me again, he asked for a meeting.

When we met, he was not the dignified person I had known. He was disheveled from sleeplessness and drink. Where was the man who had graced Durham's churches with his thoughtful slide presentations, who had lectured me about going to Sunday school and church with a number of references to "Our Savior"? What he wanted most from me was a promise not to tell, for his career and social life were built on the assumption that he was single. What I saw that day so dismayed me that I decided not to tell. This "noble" man, so high-minded and ethical, had deceived me and many others by his appearance and manner.

I wrote to John's benefactor in Africa, inquiring about his marital status. The answer reported that John indeed had a wife and children.

Still stunned by my "failure," I decided to educate myself about sexual matters. I read what was then in the library, but discovered to my dismay that most of it was lyrical; little was clinical or graphic. So after I had read book after book, I really didn't know any more than I knew before.

I was too ashamed to consult anyone until two years later, when I mentioned it to a man who was a good buddy, a chum. When I told him about my "failure," he was incredulous. I told him of my desperate efforts to solve my problem by consulting books and trying to put together what bits of conversation I had heard. When he had finally convinced himself that I was indeed relating a true account, he explained that the man in question had a serious problem. At first I didn't want to accept this explanation. After all, I had spent two years of my life beating myself over the head for many things and was reluctant to let up even that little bit. But I finally realized that I had been a victim of a hoax.

It was this period in my life—needing information and not having a good, honest source from which to get it—that led me to my unshakable belief that censorship of any kind, ignorance of any matter are the bane of human existence; that without a clear understanding of the nature of human life in all its aspects one can never fully develop his or her potential. Protect children, yes. But adults need no protection. If some few are too susceptible to certain ideas, that is the price that society will have to pay. The opposite is much worse.

My experience with John was not unique, as I then imagined. Black underclass women in general are preyed upon relentlessly. Those without a husband or a "man" are pressured by the culture around them into some sort of relationship; otherwise their femininity is called into question—openly. Men often face the same dilemma. Trying to establish a more productive life, a personally fulfilling career, is almost impossible in such circumstances. Black folk culture is fearful of and hostile to patterns of life in which one postpones or denies certain facets of life, mainly physical sex, in order to concentrate on more meaningful goals, pursuits, or endeavors. To them such a life-style is "unnatural." This cultural factor, not the absence of morals, I feel, is the root cause of the high rates of illegitimate pregnancies among black girls. The only escape available during the period prior to the sixties—and even now, in the small towns and inner cities of urban areas—is in extreme religiosity.

Still, the church is not always the haven that girls and women seek. A woman once told me of an incident in the home where she roomed. She was Holy and Sanctified, as were her landlord and his wife. As a matter of fact, he was pastor for two Holiness churches. She had lived with the couple for a number of years, and, though she never could pinpoint what the matter was, she sensed a great deal of tension between herself and the husband.

Finally, one day during an exchange of words over some minor matter, he sought to end the argument by saying, "Any woman as old as you are who doesn't have a man, you know there's something wrong with them."

She denied that there was anything wrong with her.

He said, "You're the first woman who ever lived in my house that I didn't 'cover.' "

She said, "Men who go with a lot of different women are no good in bed anyhow."

Whereupon the Holiness preacher asked, "You want to try it?"

Her answer was to walk out of the room, and soon after that she walked out of their house for good.

8

In early spring I decided to move away from my family. I found a four-room second-story apartment near the NCC campus, which I furnished sparsely with secondhand furniture from Mason's. This was my first venture at housekeeping for myself. It was a new beginning for me.

By chance Hazel, my former schoolmate, lived in the same neighborhood with her husband and son. Hazel had developed a collagen disease—a very rare ailment similar to muscular dystrophy. She and I had started in the first grade together. I remember her well, for she was very plain. She was out sick a lot, but from the first grade on, children teased her. "Shut your mouth, Hazel," they would yell, for the teacher would always tell her that. And Hazel would snap it shut. At first she used to cry when the children teased her, but then she learned to laugh. And she learned how to get back. She developed a malicious tongue with which to destroy her enemies behind their backs. But soon Hazel lost the distinction between friend and enemy, and treated everyone alike, smiling and ever so friendly to their faces, and malicious behind their backs.

I don't know why Hazel started counting me as a friend. I suspect it was that she considered me an outsider too. However, I was not the perfect friend, for I was a better student than Hazel, who was always second to me in schoolwork. Thus, she was caught between two stools. On the one hand, she needed me so that she wouldn't feel so alone in her outsidedness; on the other hand, I was the one who continuously cheated her of the position of first place that she so coveted.

Now she lay sick, and though neither of us knew it at the time, she would never get well. But what I most thought about when I sat and listened to her talk was the fact that she had no knowledge at all of her true nature. She had been a virgin when she married—at twenty-six—and she went to church on Sunday and believed in God, and it never ever occurred to her to feel that she was not a "good" girl, far better than women who stayed out late or who went to bed with men they were not married to. Helping another human being, interesting oneself in righting wrongs, working for reforms of various kinds, community service—none of these things ever crossed Hazel's mind, for they were not a part of her upbringing. I understood Hazel, for they were not a part of my upbringing either.

Hazel told me of an uproar on her job that preceded her illness. Two women in the hospital lab where she worked, both black, had been offered the chance to train as lab technicians, on the job. They had each worked in the lab for over five years. They had learned to do all the simple tests that were run by the lab. Now the civil rights movement had penetrated the hospital, and the hospital had decided to upgrade and promote some of the black workers. Hazel had a fit. The very idea, these "test tube washers" becoming lab technicians and being promoted like her! Why, she had had to study in Brooklyn, New York, for a year. Now they were going to upgrade *them.*

(Although Hazel did not refer to it, when she had finished her course of study in 1955 and applied for a job at the hospital, the head of personnel, who was the governor's sister, had done everything that she could to prevent a black woman being hired. It was only when one of the senior physicians threatened to resign on the spot that the hospital had hired her.)

Hazel was genuinely upset, and I understood. She had worked hard to put distance between herself and the two lab workers, and though after five years on the job they probably knew more than Hazel did when she was certified, and though they were colleagues, working in a tiny space not much larger than a kitchen, and though they had lunch together every day, she resented another black sharing her *status.* And I understood.

The "only black" syndrome would get worse as integration became more of a reality. The "only black" frequently fought off any attempt to add more blacks on a job, slot, position, whatever.

Black people under segregation lived in a terrible city at the bottom of a deep and bitter sea. Worse yet, like some species of piranha turned on itself, they tore and rent each other. The blacks themselves knew this and, every black mother in the

South taught her child the following folktale, the first one they ever learned:

> A man set down a bucket of crabs and went off and left them, confident that none of them would get out of the bucket. They didn't, for each time one got near the top, all the other crabs reached up and pulled him back down. Black people are like that.

I understand now some of the things about Hazel's personality that I was so unsympathetic with at the time. For example, I never could understand why someone who had been a constant reader in elementary and high school stopped reading anything. In fact, it was she who first talked to me of books when we were growing up, for her people lived on an estate, working for one of the wealthiest families in the region, and she grew up with the daughters of these rich people, reading the books that they read and listening to the radio programs that they liked. It was Hazel who came to school and told about the fairy tales on "Let's Pretend" so vividly that eventually I was persuaded to listen to them and grew to like them. She and I were two of the steadiest readers in the small library that lined the walls of our classroom. We often traded good stories. That is, if she read a book and liked it and told me the story, often I would read it, and then I would do the same for her. We traded stories right on through the ninth grade. And we both liked "Lux Radio Theatre" and loved to talk about it the next day. But by the time we were in the tenth grade and fifteen years old, Hazel started to change; she didn't talk about stories so much anymore.

She went to NCC for two years and then went away to Brooklyn, to study medical technology for a year and a half, and then she changed even more. For when she came back to North Carolina and started working in a hospital, she never again mentioned a book, a story, a movie. She confined her conversation solely to the past, and by the age of twenty-five a lot of her sentences started with, "Remember the time when

. . ." And her conversations would be filled with reminiscences of former classmates. I suspect that incessant gossip came to fill the need that had once been served by reading *Sue Barton, Private Nurse* and listening to the story of Bluebeard.

But what had happened? Why did Hazel do this—completely eliminate anything even remotely current or contemporary from her life? The only reason that I can think of was that she wanted to get married. And looking around realistically at what was available, she knew that she would have a chance only with a member of the black working class. And since such a man would be suspicious of and possibly hostile to any show of learning or cultivation on his wife's part, Hazel deliberately set about erasing it from her pattern of life. And it worked. She met Paul and they married, and to all intents and purposes it was a good marriage. A dark muscular man, he worked hard as a construction worker during the week and went to the Baptist church on Sunday wearing his black suit, for he was an usher. And eventually they had a little boy. They bought land in Durham County and started planning to build. So it evened out. If Hazel had given up some vital part of herself to marry, she had gotten some solid rewards in return. She seemed happy enough with the bargain she had struck, until she got sick and knew that she would never get well.

It was then that she had time to think on her life and what she had denied herself and the rewards that it had brought her, and she became unhappy with the bargain she had made.

For some reason, during her long slow illness Hazel became increasingly concerned that I was unmarried; she seemed to be determined to do something about it. She would sit, her eyes even more extraordinarily large, for her face and frame were slowly wasting away, and patiently inquire as to my love life. I had none. "Then what about John Doe? He's not married and I could arrange . . ." and I would demur, for I wasn't interested. "Well," she would counter, "Paul knows a man on his job, a bricklayer, and he makes five dollars an hour, and the other night he and I were talking and we thought that we'd

111

invite both of you to dinner . . ." And I would demur and she would persist.

As the months passed, Hazel started doing some strange things. The first I knew of it was when one of her former colleagues at the hospital came up and congratulated me on my recent marriage. Recent marriage? I didn't know what she was talking about. I went along with her, never saying yes, or no, trying to find out what was behind it. Who was it I was supposed to have married? But I couldn't glean that information. But she did tell me that Hazel had told her. And I was left to wonder. Why in the world would Hazel make up a story out of whole cloth, just invent a husband, which she knew I didn't have? And knowing Hazel, I knew that she had told half of Durham by now.

In the coming weeks I received a query here and there about my alleged marriage, and the source of the story was always the same. Yet, when I visited Hazel, she didn't mention it to me. What seemed to be at the root of it was Hazel's deep anger that she, at such a young age, was stricken with an incurable illness, while I at the same age walked around. But what was even more infuriating to her was that she had paid the price, she had crushed down all signs of intellectual curiosity in herself, contenting herself with watching television with her husband and going to work every day and to church on Sunday, thinking that that was the only way, while I, always alone, without support, had a measure of freedom that she didn't have.

And that was the sticking point, that there was a chance, a very slight chance, that in my wanderings around out there I might get away scot-free. I might somehow survive without paying the price that she, and so many black women, had paid. And she was certain that it was willful on my part. Hazel and a lot of other black women used to tell me, "You could get married if you really wanted to." And beneath the surface concern, I heard the anger. "Join us. This is our lot in life. Who are you to try escape? This is the way it's been. This is the way it is. Everybody has some pain in life; that's the way life is. There's no need trying to duck and dodge your share. Come on in with us." But though I smiled and agreed to their faces, inside I said, "No. Not me. Never. Never."

The summer of 1962 was very hot. My upstairs apartment turned into an oven, and in the late afternoon, when the sun moved to the front of the house, I spent a lot of time on the metal porch on the roof at the back. The days had a pattern that in itself was not unpleasant. In the morning I drove to Chapel Hill, where I took a course in English—not for any particular reason, but just to keep a hand in, so to speak. After class I went to the library and stayed there until I was through with the next day's assignments. Then I drove home in the hot early afternoon sun. Often I would not even go upstairs until I had visited Hazel. I would sit with her a half hour or so, then go home and put on supper.

Supper was nearly always beef curry. My friend Gupta, who taught physics at Duke University, had taught me to pre-pare it; it was new, something different, and I liked it. Even though he was a Hindu, Gupta rather proudly announced to everybody that he ate beef. I think in some way it was linked in his mind to his scientific training. I had a feeling that it wasn't that he liked beef, but that he had to prove that he was not subject to nonscientific superstitions. The only problem was that it took so long to prepare that, by the time I was fin-ished, my already hot apartment was unbearable. I would take a pound and a half to two pounds of ground beef, salt and pepper it to taste, and add a heaping tablespoon of curry pow-der. Then I would put it in the deep well on the electric stove and let it cook slowly. It was important that all fat be scooped out the minute it appeared in the pot, so that the meat would not fry or stick together. That is why the temperature at all times had to be low. Most of the time, the dish would take three or four hours to prepare, but when it was done, each grain of beef stood by itself, the whole being a dark grayish color, and it was absolutely delicious.

Sometimes, in addition to the curry, I would open a can of

black-eyed peas, pour off half of the water it was packed in, add a large chopped onion and a tablespoon of curry and a fourth of a cup of oil, pour it all in the frying pan, and let it cook until the onions were done. Gupta showed me how to fix it and told me the name of it was "lobia."

Then, in the early evening, about seven o'clock, I would cut up fresh onions and cucumber and tomatoes for a salad, and around seven-thirty or eight, Gupta would come. I would hear his footsteps on the iron stairs, and soon he would knock. We'd set up a table out on the porch, and while we ate he'd tell me the news of the day. After supper Gupta would wash the dishes—I don't mind cooking, but I do hate to wash dishes—and then we'd talk. The talk went on until it got dark and the stars came out. I had to keep a watch on the time, for the last bus was at eleven, and if he missed it Gupta would have to walk the seven or eight miles to Duke. And though he wasn't afraid and walked it many a night, I still wondered about such a frail man out alone that late at night, particularly now that Durham had become a racial battleground and either side might attack him. But he didn't seem to mind, and if I forgot to check the clock it often would be nearly midnight before he left.

Sometimes after supper we would visit Hazel, or we would walk the four or five blocks to the College Inn, or go to a nightclub two blocks away. But often we just sat and talked.

I used to think what an incongruous pair Gupta and I made walking down Fayetteville Street to the College Inn. But I was glad, for I wanted the world to know that I could have a friend. He was short and dark and unbelievably thin, despite the fact that he ate meat. His arms were skeletal, like matchsticks. His scrawniness, coupled with the fact that he had started to gray early, made him seem much older than he was. The fact that he wore glasses, which he perpetually had to push back up on his nose, didn't help matters any either.

I looked forward to the atmosphere of the Inn, where it was always brightly lit, very clean, and the jukebox played all the time. I suspect that the air-conditioning at the Inn, however, was the strongest drawing card for me, for my apartment was very hot and that, coupled with the fact that I had spent the morning in a hot classroom and had driven home in the hot sun and had been hot all the afternoon, made me look with longing to the chill of the College Inn. There Gupta and I would have sodas and talk about nothing in particular.

My favorite spot, however, was a nightclub nearby. Once or twice during the week, and on weekends, there was live music there. And I loved it. I like to hear a singer. Instrumental music I appreciate, but singing I love. If the singer has a good voice, and if the words are good, and if the singer sounds as if he or she also believes them, I can listen all night long and never get tired. Something in the blend of voice and words and meaning touches me in such a way that I forget what I am or where or who, and I become more spirit than body.

Often there was a combo there from Chapel Hill that played on Wednesday nights. They had two singers: a man, plump and yellow, with a high pompadour and a sweet voice; and a black girl in her late teens, who was very voluptuous but too plump, and who had a nice, but not rich enough voice. They would sing and sing, and while others at their tables talked and clinked their glasses, I sat entranced; I never wanted to go until the last song had been sung.

However, as the days, then weeks, passed and June faded into July, I found myself becoming increasingly fatigued in the relationship. In other words, I was tired of it, and I wanted to end it. Yet I couldn't let myself think such thoughts. For wasn't Gupta a very nice person, spending hours explaining to me the various theories of physics, including the spinning theory, which he explained so thoroughly that for two whole days I think I could have written it up on an examination? One night we were sitting on the porch very late, and Gupta pointed out a satellite to me. I was interested to see it, for though I had read of sightings, I had never seen one myself. What surprised me about it was that it was not streaking across the sky like a meteor, but seemed to me to be backing up and turning around. Gupta explained that effect to me.

Such an intensely platonic relationship tired me, though I was ashamed to admit it. Others didn't think it was platonic, I knew, for some teased me about it. I suppose I should have felt self-righteous and either thought or said, How dare they . . . ? I felt a little of that, to be sure, but mainly I felt a keen sort of hurt that someone who came every night, seven nights a week, plainly had no physical interest in me. Yet still he came, and I suspected that what Gupta wanted was sympathy and support, for he felt that he had been badly treated at Duke. But he didn't want to go home without a degree—he feared loss of face—and so far no other university had made him a firm offer.

The days dragged by and I kept up my cheerful greetings when he came, but I was tired, tired, tired. And the days continued the same. A second summer session started, and I enrolled in more courses. I continued to visit Hazel, listening to her talk about the past as though she were an old woman, yet she was barely thirty. And preparing supper for Gupta and listening, listening to him. And the heat never let up.

Gupta was very excited by the civil rights movement and spent a lot of time talking about it, trying to find out as much as he could. At first I thought that his great interest stemmed from his knowledge of Gandhi's teachings, but I soon learned that he had personal reasons as well.

A powerful professor felt that Gupta would be a good high-school or junior-college physicist, but that he was not suited for a university post. Gupta wrote to a former professor of his in India, and at an international meeting of physicists the Indian professor protested to the American professor about the latter's failure to perceive Gupta's abilities. The American brought this exchange back to Duke and, as the saying goes, the fat was in the fire, and Gupta had to start looking around for somewhere to go. So he stayed in Durham for the summer, having completed his preliminary work but not yet having received an appointment.

Thus I was relieved when one evening Gupta told me that a

New England university had given him a grant. After that the summer became easier. He left at the end of August, and in September I began another year of teaching at North Carolina College.

9

Late one Sunday night when it was cold—it was really early Monday morning—I woke up. Something was wrong, but I didn't know what. I lay suspended between sleep and waking for a while, trying to figure out what it was. I couldn't get my thoughts together. Finally, it penetrated: there was a sound at my front door. I didn't look at the clock, but I guessed that it was about three or four a.m. I listened some more, and as my head began to clear, I realized that it was someone knocking. I quickly discarded the idea that something was wrong at home in Wildwood, for I had a telephone, and if something bad had happened, they would have called me. The knocking continued, a steady pounding. Perhaps it was someone looking for whoever used to live in the apartment. I sat on the bed and tried to decide what to do. Maybe if I didn't go to the door, whoever it was would go away. But the knocking had been going on a long time and showed no sign of stopping. Perhaps I would just go to the door and find out who it was and tell them they had made a mistake. That way the knocking would stop, for by now it had been going on so long that my land-lord, who lived downstairs, had probably heard it. I didn't want to get up and was a little afraid, but I always fastened the storm door securely when I came in so no one could sud-denly barge in. So I decided to go to the door.

I didn't turn on my bedroom light; I could see well enough by the light in the hall. The knocking continued, steady and muffled. I peered through the venetian blinds of the win-dow—the door was partially glass—and saw a figure standing there on the upstairs front porch. I didn't turn on the porch light because I didn't want to attract the attention of the neighbors.

"Who is it?" I asked, partly cracking the door.

He gave the name of a man who once had been an acquaintance. I had taken him for a friend, but he had turned out otherwise. But now what did he want and what was he doing at my apartment at that time of night? I wanted the noise to stop and I didn't want to turn on the porch light, so I unhooked the storm door and let him in. I still couldn't see clearly, for I didn't turn on the light in the first room, but led the way saying, "We'll go in here," and started across the many-cornered hall to the room that served as a sitting room. I was talking all the time. "Whatever in the world are you doing here? What do you want?"

It must have been the silence that first came through to me. He wasn't saying anything. Then there was something else that came through; I don't quite know what, but when it did, I turned to look full face at him. For what seemed to be a thousand years I looked at him. He wasn't who he said he was!

Standing in my hallway at four in the morning was a man I had never seen before. I thought about a hundred stories I had read about women found slain with no sign of forcible entry, and now I knew what had happened to some of them. I don't know what expression was on my face, but the stranger shrank back from it almost as if I had hit him. Then I knew that I had a chance. I started pushing and railing against this terror, who was very dark and had on a dark raincoat. He resisted but still allowed himself to be pushed back, back into the front room, back toward the door. We must have been a strange tableau, for I was embracing him, not to draw him nearer but to drag and push him to the door.

I heard a voice high and far away, and I realized that it was mine—I was screaming, but I didn't recognize it or really hear what it was saying. Finally the terror was at the door and I shoved and pushed him out on the porch. He went without

118

striking back. I wonder even now about that. I sometimes think this stranger was just drunk enough to do something evil, like coming in on me in disguise, but not drunk enough not to know that he was in the wrong.

No sooner had I pushed him out the door than he ran down the steps and started ringing the bell on the back porch downstairs. I was weak with the horror of the night, but I went down the inside stairs to try to stop him, for the noise would wake my landlord. I don't know why I didn't just ignore it, but I couldn't think at all. I had ceased to be able to think ahead and was just reacting to the terror of the moment.

Enraged at being forced out and seeming to feel that he had a right to come in, the man continued to ring the downstairs bell and bang on the door. The racket awakened my landlord, and he came out on the back porch. He yelled to the intruder, but it only seemed to enrage him more. Finally, my landlord put on the light, and through the dusty glass and the screen I saw the horror run off.

Shaken, I blurted some explanation to my landlord. I went upstairs to bed, but I didn't sleep. I tried to figure out what had happened.

Still later, in the early morning hours, the terror returned and started knocking, knocking on my upstairs porch. I lay out of breath, mouth dry and heart beating. Then I heard steps going away. By then it was dawn, light outside.

At that moment I wanted to break up housekeeping—go back to live with my mother—but I wouldn't, I couldn't. For if I gave up now and admitted that I had made a mistake, everybody would crow, "See, she can't do anything but keep her head in a book." And my relatives would smile their smug smiles that said, "So you're back. I told you so."

That was not the end. On the next Sunday night, and several Sundays after that, around three or four in the morning, the knocking would start. A steady, unhurried knocking that said, Open the door, I have a right to come in. And I lay there thinking, Why me?

And the knocking would go on until the man lost interest for the night and went away, satisfied that in some way he had hurt me. For the game was not to come in; he knew that I would never open the door again; the game was to punish me for having rejected him.

I hadn't wanted to call in the police because I didn't want to become involved with them. But the more I thought about it, the more I realized that the man plainly enjoyed harassing me and was planning to keep it up forever, free from fear of any reprisal on my part. I wrung and I twisted, but there was no way out of it. Either I would act or I would suffer. It was unfair, it was wrong, but there was no one to right that wrong except me. Finally I decided. The next time I had a visit from him, I would call the police.

That night, around three o'clock, the steady, steady knocking started. I got up and sat on the bed and by the light from the hall slowly dialed the police number. My hands were shaking so that I had to place my finger in the slot carefully to turn the dial. The police answered and I reported a prowler, then lay back down to see what would happen. It was out of my hands. In a few minutes, I heard a heavier, more authoritative knock. I pulled on a robe and went to the door. There were two black policemen standing on opposite sides of a slender black man with a part in his hair and a slight pompadour. He had on a white shirt and grayish-looking trousers.

The police officers told me that when they had asked what he was doing there, he had said that he had left his raincoat on a previous visit. I said that I had been bothered for weeks by someone who came late on Sunday nights and knocked on my door and that I was prepared to go to the police station and sign a complaint. The officers said that that wasn't necessary.

The last I saw of my intruder, he was seated in the police car, a dazed look on his face. He was surprised, evidently feeling that the game had been perfected, never once thinking that I would call the police. I went back to bed and, for the first time in weeks, slept without dreaming. I never heard anything more from my prowler. I didn't know what happened to him, I never knew his name, and though I can speculate as to who he was and why he came, I still can't be sure. But one thing I learned that night, a thing that unfortunately I had to learn over and over, was that failure to respond to a gross wrong was a sure way to insure that it will continue. Life has taught me that many, many times, but somehow I keep forgetting.

Part

THREE

10

Back in 1955, during my last year as an undergraduate student at NCC, I had been deeply moved by news broadcasts showing empty buses on the streets of Montgomery, Alabama. I felt a strong surge of pride one evening when I saw an interview with a bus driver, a young white man, sitting in his bus, who said, "They come to the door in their wrappers and bedroom shoes and look out when I pass, but nobody gets on the bus." Then the television camera followed his route around the city. At street corners, in front yards, and at certain downtown places, clusters of blacks waited for the car pools that would take them where they were going. The empty bus rolled on through the black section and didn't pick up a single passenger. The solidarity was a beautiful thing to me, and for the first time I had hope, because it seemed to me that in the past people of my ethnic group had continually fought each other, put each other down, and refused to help each other. I had lived under segregation all my life, and I felt that it would last forever because we blacks were too divided among ourselves to stop it.

I had been wrong. For now the civil rights movement that had started at a lunch counter in Greensboro, North Carolina, in 1960, had reached Durham. Demonstrations flared for several nights: newspapers and television programs were full of them. Overcoming my deep fear, I decided to follow my other bent, my inclination to be on the spot where things were happening. History was being made, and I wanted to be there to observe it.

One night I went uptown to see. There were lights, lights everywhere, cars racing up and down, crowds moving through the street. It looked like Christmas, but at Christmas it was cold and people were wrapped up in garments and they had little puffs of smoke in front of their mouths. Tonight it was hot and people had no coats on. And the noise, and cars, cars everywhere, and sirens from far away. It was a parade. It was a celebration. It was a holiday. But it was not a festival. It was anger. The whites were angry, and the blacks were determined. And the sirens never stopped wailing.

I approached a spot where a lot of people were gathered. It was a shallow arena, one side facing a main thoroughfare. It was the parking lot in front of the Sears store on Main Street; artificial light was everywhere. It didn't look like a parking lot anymore, for on all three sides there were people near the edge looking in and down. They had to look down, for the parking lot was shaped like a shallow bowl. Once the cars entered, they went down, down. There, in the lowest part of the lot, where the cars would be in the daytime, were two figures locked back to back, their arms joined.

They were black, their bodies young and muscular. They had short hair. One had on purple corduroy pants and a cutout sweatshirt. The other wore a short-sleeved shirt and nondescript trousers. They were staging a sit-in. Locked together back to back as one, they could not be broken apart, and they would be hard to move. There was so much light that it looked like day, but if you looked at the sky, the sky was black. If you looked at the people around the wall, they were white and black. The whites were shouting hate slogans. I had once seen a movie set in ancient Rome, during the early days of Christianity, and I had watched the Emperor turn his thumb down, meaning "Slay the Christians," while all the

126

people roared. Tonight they were roaring, but it wasn't, "Slay the Christians." It was, "Run over them!"

A car had been backed up to the young black men, its back-up lights glowing like red eyes; the driver was inundating them with carbon monoxide, the exhaust from the car. But the young men were holding fast, and at every emission, at every race of the motor, the whites yelled, "Run over them! Run over them! Back over them! Kill them! Run over them!"

I paused, frozen by the scene. There were whites of all types standing around—people in from the country, city slickers from the town, men, women, and children—and these were neighbors. They saw them every day. They delivered the paper, or they delivered the milk, or they came to fix the television antenna. They bagged their groceries in the grocery store or they delivered their mail. But tonight they were the enemy, and the whites yelled, "Run over them! Kill them!"

The blacks were also standing there, around the low guardrail, and they were cheering on the young black men, yelling words of encouragement so that the two of them would know that they were not alone.

It seemed as though time stood still while the car engine raced and its red back-up eyes glowed, and the crowd shouted, "Run over them! Run over them! Kill them!" And the young men stayed locked together and would not move. The scene remained frozen. The engine raced; the crowd shouted; the young men did not move.

The sirens never stopped wailing. I left the young men locked in their unmovable stance and moved on up Main Street from the parking lot, the sounds of "Run over them! Run over them! Kill them!" still in my ears. I prayed that they would be all right—and moved toward the center of the town, ducking and dodging clusters of people.

One block away I picked up the sound of *clump, clump, clump.* A revival meeting, a church meeting in the middle of the town? But it was not a church meeting. A long, long line of people was coming down the street, just at the edge of the sidewalk, and it was swaying and moving with many, many feet, like a giant multicolored centipede. It was linked together hand in hand, and it was going around the block, and this pulsating organism was saying, "Freedom, freedom, freedom!"

The organism had many voices, but they all sounded as one. It had many feet, but they all moved as one pair. And it had many colors. It was mainly black, but it was white, too. It was mainly young, but it was mature, too. It was moving with a purpose, and it was not dismayed. It shouted, "Freedom, freedom, freedom!" and it went up the street and around the block, and there was no break. I stood in the street to watch, among the other blacks who were watching too. The voice never stopped chanting, "Freedom, freedom, freedom, freedom!" Police sirens wailed, but this long line of people didn't stop, not even when a Trailways bus passed with other people, arms out of the window, yelling, on their way to jail. There were so many of them that the police had loaded them into a bus to bring them to jail. And crowds moved through the streets, and cars honked, and police sirens wailed, and this multicolored, multifooted organism yelled, "Freedom, freedom!" The arms reached out of the bus, the people, yelling, "Yeah . . . ah . . . yeah . . . ah." And I walked on, bumping into people who seemed to be as dazed as I was. There was electricity everywhere, and I was drawn to it and had to move on.

One observer reported the following scene:

A light-skinned black man and a brown-haired white woman knelt on the sidewalk in front of the Criterion Theater. A long Cadillac screeched to a halt in front of the theater. and a portly white man and a dyed-blond woman got out and came and stood over the demonstrators.

"Move!" the man said. The kneelers said nothing.

"Move, I said!"

They said nothing.

The portly man unwrapped an object that he had been carrying in a tablecloth. It was a double-barreled shotgun. He had come to protect his movie house, with its sex pictures, from the threat of college students and other believers in the American dream.

The kneeling man and woman said nothing, ignoring the shotgun, a tableau of the American South in the early 1960s. What had brought this about? Black people had changed their position and the white man's world had cracked. And he came with a shotgun wrapped in a white tablecloth, trying to put it back together again.

Betty, a black college girl, entered Harvey's, a restaurant with long plate-glass windows that looked out on Main Street. She entered alone; she had come to get her supper. The other patrons hurried away at once, but one man was adamant. He would stay. All the other customers had left by the time she sat down.

The manager ran to her. "Get out! Get out of here! What are you doing in here? Get out of here!"

Betty said, "Haven't I got a right to be here?"

"No, you haven't."

"I just want to eat."

"No, you don't."

"Yes, I do. Here, I've got the money."

"Get out of here! Get out before I call the police!"

And the one remaining patron was so upset that he put his napkin down and yelled at Betty, "See! See! You spoiled my supper. Now what are you going to do about it? You spoiled my supper!"

I walked on. In the basement of the courthouse, in the yard in front of the courthouse, were people, people everywhere. Electricity was in the air, and noise, shouting, police sirens, the cries of "Freedom!" across the street and down the block, and the buses in the yard, and people yelling in unison, "Yeah . . ." On the top floor was the jail. Some of the white prisoners who were unsympathetic were throwing things down on the blacks. One student reported that the policemen didn't know what to do. How could they book all these people? One policeman gave a sheet of paper to a group of students and said, "Here, book yourselves, then." And the night was bright and many sleepwalkers were on the street. To some it was their awakening from a nightmare.

I moved on, touching a wanderer here and there, rebounding from him, then continuing to an area two blocks below the courthouse, where I stopped and looked, fascinated. Coming across the railroad tracks behind Kress's were people from another part of town, a black part, and they said, "Are they hurting the boys and girls? Where are those motherfuckers?" These were the violent ones, the ones who knew how to strike back when they were struck, the ones who didn't go to church on Sunday, who were not aware of Martin Luther King, Jr. They didn't want the blacks hurt, and though they would never go to school, and though they had a low status in the black community, they too had a sense of solidarity and were coming to see what was happening. They were not for turning the other cheek; they were saying, "Kill the motherfuckers."

I was scared, for the only reason blood hadn't flowed tonight was that the blacks on the street had been nonviolent, absorbing injury. But the black women and men on the railroad tracks were the rock-and-bottle throwers, and they weren't planning to absorb anything.

I moved on. Sometimes I thought I saw lightning. The atmosphere seemed heavy, but it was not threatening to rain; it was the sheer energy that had been released in the downtown section. All the forces had come together, and they were acting like an electric shock on me. I had long been a sleepwalker, and this was a time of awakening. This is a great movement, I thought, but what can I do?

I walked on through the town, and across the tracks, out of the downtown section. But my perception of the world would never be the same again.

The Durham *Morning Herald* said, "Six Hundred Arrested, Mainly College Students." Some of them were arrested as many as three times during the night.

The mother of one of the students was interviewed. "How do you feel about your child being in jail?"

She said, "I am overjoyed."

Her child was fifteen years old.

130

There was to be a mass meeting that night at St. Joseph's
A.M.E. Church. I decided to go.

It was a warm evening. There was a royal-blue sky with a
few white clouds fluttering across. The church was a large red
brick structure. Churches are the dominant feature in black
communities, and there are many, many of them, some right
around the corner from each other. Every congregation has its
church, and sometimes when a few dissident members get unhappy, they move out and call a minister and build another
church.

The movement took turns in meeting, now in the Baptist
church, now in the Methodist church, now in another church.
The only requirement was a large auditorium, for the whole
town was stirred up and everybody came out to hear the
speaker.

The meeting was at eight. At seven the church was full.
They started by singing "We Shall Overcome."

The whole church was swaying. The black and white young
civil-righters were sitting in front, arms linked, swaying to the
music. The song continued.

The mood was one of high excitement. I myself felt glad to
think that I was part of a movement. I was older than the
movement, outside of it, but I was black and a part of it!

I wasn't familiar with the new words. These were old
church songs that they had put new words to. The youngsters
were a bit too enthusiastic, but they had accomplished what
my generation had never accomplished—unity for a purpose.

In the midst of the "We shall overcomes" I looked around.
There were working people fresh out of the factories, professorial types, lots and lots of young people; they sang and
waited and sang and waited.

It was time to start. People were standing around the back,
against walls. First, there was prayer. You prayed for strength
to forgive your enemies. Then there was Scriptures reading,
and the passage spoke of determination and of God's help for
his people. A song came after that. "Hold on, hold on, keep
your hands on the plough, hold on." Then the speaker of the

131

hour, Floyd McKissick, an attorney, came, and he was a fiery speaker, recounting the injuries that black people have suffered in this country, touching a chord that everybody could respond to. "Amen, brother!" He was not a preacher, but he knew the stops, and when he played them the whole congregation sounded like a giant organ, roaring back at him. He ended his speech with, "Now there comes a time when we must throw off this yoke, we must stand up as free men, we must demand our rights!"

At every pause the audience yelled, "Amen! Bravo! Yeah! Bravo! Amen! Bravo! Tell it, tell it, tell it!" Then at a fervent pitch, McKissick reached into his pocket and pulled out a note, and he said, "You are now welcome at the Greenlight Restaurant." And everybody shouted, "Yeah!" And I shouted along with them, though I wondered at sixteen hundred people yelling happily because they could now go to a hamburger stand. But then I realized the significance of it. Sixteen hundred people and others like them all around, all over the city, all over the state, all over the South, had forced a wedge into the law in every town and hamlet in the South. And that was something to cheer about. It wasn't the hamburger and the french fries and the cold drinks; it was the fact that by being united they had succeeded in overcoming the intransigent racial policies of the region.

A few nights later I went to another meeting at Mt. Vernon Baptist Church. I observed the incongruity of this huge brick structure with stained-glass windows, high on a hilltop, surrounded by a huddle of shacks. It looked like a huge cathedral in a tiny French town, with the little houses in its shadow.

Dark-suited deacons and church ladies in crepe dresses and flower-garden hats pushed and shoved to get in. The networks in New York had been made aware of the situation in Durham, and had sent a television crew to record it for their Friday-night news program. Therefore everybody was coming, black and white young people, leaders of the civil rights movement, ministers of the town—some active supporters of the movement, and some not—and the white power structure,

132

represented by the mayor. Everybody was going to show up.

The meeting was to be at eight. At six-thirty the church was full. I was with a group of ladies and gentlemen, shoving and pushing in a very un-Christian-like manner, trying to get into the church. I also felt several pinches and pulls in places I shouldn't have felt them, but when I looked around I saw only sober-faced deacons. But I persevered, got in, and stood against the wall.

"We shall overcome . . . hold on, keep your hand on the plough, hold on. . . ." All the old spirituals that I had learned as a child were sung with a new beat, a new intonation, and a new hope in this congregation. Inside it was hotter than outside. There were so many people, and it was well-lighted, for the TV cameras panned the room. People were a little more spruced up and a little more enthusiastic than they had been on the nights when no network people were here. And among the speakers on the stand was a thin man with a red carnation in his buttonhole. He was the mayor.

The service followed the same pattern as the last one. There was a reading from the Scriptures and there was a speech. The mayor promised the services of his office to help heal the tensions in the community. But the mayor was not talking for everybody, as the coming days ahead proved.

Headlines screamed out: A HUNDRED MORE ARRESTED. TWO HUNDRED MORE ARRESTED. JAIL CELLS CROWDED. Students talked of filth in the jails, inadequate food, overcrowded facilities. The night air of many Southern towns was pierced by sirens. Demonstrators, anxious parents, hostile whites, happy blacks, angry blacks. Freedom was in the air, and there were those who were frightened by it, those who welcomed it, and those who hated it. But to be alive, to be a participant, to be an observer when history was being made was very exciting to me.

I thought about what I could do, how I could make a contribution. I had heard about the picketing of movie houses, and since I was a movie fan myself, I thought perhaps I would start there. One night I went to a storefront near the Palms Restaurant and put my hands up and swore an oath of nonviolence.

So at night I started to work around the edges of the movement, feeling out of place because I was older than the students, and also because they were believers in a dream that had never been real for me.

The Center Theater, a movie house, was on a corner, built at an angle. One side was bounded by a main thoroughfare and the other side by a short street. The front of the theater projected outward, joining the two streets, but really facing neither one. The "white" side was on the big street. On the little street was a small door marked COLORED ENTRANCE. White people went through a lobby with red carpet and a ticket taker seated just behind the glass doors. Black people stepped through the "colored entrance," bought a ticket at the foot of the stairs, and went immediately up to the second-floor level. There they could sit and look down on the white people.

In the eastern part of the state there had recently been trouble at a movie house. Some white boys decided to teach the blacks a lesson and stood up to throw things at the "colored balcony." They forgot that they were at a strategic disadvantage. Their opponents had the high ground, and flying objects rained down so intensely on the whites that the police had to be called in.

This movie house was one of the two in Durham that admitted "colored" patrons. The others didn't admit blacks at all. If the movie you wanted to see came to one of the all-white movie houses, that was just your tough luck. Apparently this arrangement had troubled the conscience of no one. It was the custom. That perhaps the black population didn't have such high regard for this custom never seemed to occur to the owners and patrons of the movie houses. Thus they were unprepared for the assault when it came.

I joined the picket line in front of the movie house. When a car pulled up my stomach tightened, as if someone were squeezing my intestines. My chest felt funny, as though I was trying to force down a liquid that was too hot. Would they call me names? My legs felt tense. I thought of how easily a bullet could pierce flesh, and wondered how it would feel. Would it make me hot all over or would I feel cold? Knife victims felt cold, so my biology teacher once said, or was it thirsty? Even though I was with ten other people walking up and down in front of the theater carrying signs, I felt completely alone. If "they" were in the car and if they had a gun, I would die alone, alone in the bright artificial light—and all for a seat in a dark movie house, where they flashed pictures on a shiny screen and faraway places came alive.

I loved the movies, even though I never saw myself on the screen. For two hours the world was filled with mystery and romance. If it was a detective story, I ran with both the criminal and the detective through the whole picture. I loved the chase. Whichever one was running at the time, that was the one I ran with. I loved the sea, and a shot of an enormous expanse of water without any ship or anything on it made me smile with joy. No matter what happened to me, whether I lived or died, whether I was unhappy or not, the sea was there. It was something unchanging in a world of flux.

I liked the movies best in the summer. That was when the contrast with the outside world was greatest. Coming in out of a hot, hot Southern sun, I liked to go into the cool pitch-blackness of a movie house early in the day. There I felt as if I were in a pitcher of cold lemonade and icy tingles went through my body. There were few people there, and soon I blocked them out of my mind; then there was just me and the picture.

On the picket line there was artificial light everywhere. To me, born and raised in the country, artificial light always carried a special significance. Perhaps it was because I rarely saw it, except at Christmas, with the street lamps and store windows lit up, or when I went to a basketball game at the armory or to the movies at night.

Night to me meant dark. At home in Wildwood when there was no moon you actually couldn't see anything at night beyond the front porch. You would know there was a car passing because of the headlight it threw and red light it left behind. It looked like a black streak whispering on soft tires down the road. Sonny, the son of the white hunchback who lived around the corner up on the hill from Wildwood, used to drive his car at night with no lights. One night in Wildwood it passed me so quietly and so fast that it nearly scared me to death. I thought of it as a death car. It was completely invisible until it was right on me. Then it was gone, swift and dark. It threw no shadows.

But the night here was lighted. There was nowhere to hide. People were staying away from the movie theater. Those who did want trouble came to harass the demonstrators, not to see the picture.

I had never felt so vulnerable in all my life. There I stood in the naked light. All around me were those who were hostile and some who were just standing. Across the street a white woman and her two children paraded with the Confederate flag. A boy of about thirteen carried the Stars and Bars. They were counterpickets. In front of the theater two white men talked loudly to each other. I caught the word "nigger" and other obscenities. Across the street several strangers paused. They were from out of town. I didn't know how I knew, I just knew. They were looking on, interested. One said to another, "See the demonstrators." He looked like a basketball coach and the tall young men around him seemed to be players.

The picketers had "observers," those whose job it was to watch and report what was going on. But I didn't see the observers. It was hard enough to keep a steady walk in line carrying a sign, walking twenty paces west, then turning and walking twenty paces east, then turning and walking twenty paces west, then turning and walking twenty paces east, all the time observing the street. Suppose someone came along and fired shots. There were no policemen in sight. And even if there were, I'd be dead, and what good would policemen do then? Then I looked at the athletic young men who were harassing the pickets, laughing, knowing full well that they could harass as much as they pleased. Not only were the police not going to do anything to them, they were also not about to prevent anything. Then there were the people on the street. What were their intentions? Did they mean trouble? Walking back and forth, back and forth. Where were the observers? A car pulled up. Were they going to call out bad names? Suppose they had guns and they started to shoot? What was I going to do? I looked covertly to the side. A car had stopped at the red light. Nobody said anything. No gun protruded from the car. After an eternity the car moved again. Safe this time.

Another car. I had turned and was moving away from it. My mind played the same record, but with another variation. Would I be shot in the back or would one of the harassers hit me on the back of my head and knock me down so I wouldn't see who had done it? There was no policeman in sight and no observer. But I heard the red light click to green, and soon the cars were moving west. Would this night never end?

It was an oblong box, not much bigger than his hand. And he held it up in front of my eyes. For one heartstopping moment I thought, I don't want to die in the United States, in North Carolina, in Durham, in a flood of artificial light—for a movie. But it didn't go off. It was a camera, and he was holding it in front of my eyes and taking pictures. But I didn't see a flash. I wondered what kind of camera it was. I was so relieved that it didn't go off that I kept my pace with the others, who also didn't respond to the man with the camera. But he kept pace too, walking backward in time with my step so that he remained slightly ahead of me, moving backward as I moved, always taking pictures. Would this night never end? Finally, I turned and saw another line coming. They were our replacements. My first night as a picket was over.

My next picketing was done fifteen miles away, in Chapel Hill, several days later. The Dairy Bar was on a corner, the long part facing Franklin Street, the main street, up on a little knoll. It was on the main thoroughfare, but it was four or five blocks from the main downtown section. The short side of the Dairy Bar was on a street in a black neighborhood. That was the side the blacks were supposed to enter, where the stand-up counter was. The sit-down tables were on the long side, where the white people went in.

The manager probably thought it would cause less conflict if he put the tables very far away from the stand-up counter, so that no blacks would sit down at one of them, even by accident. Blacks could, however, stand and eat at the counter. That was protocol in Chapel Hill. Blacks stood up and ate. Whites had the privilege of sitting down if they chose. The only place where a black could sit down was an establishment that served blacks only.

So the black residents of the neighborhood came and went through the side door, buying fresh milk, ice cream, hamburgers, hot dogs, and milkshakes, while the whites from other neighborhoods came in to buy fresh milk and to sit and eat ice cream, hot dogs, hamburgers, and milkshakes.

It was decided to picket the Dairy Bar, and somehow I found myself one Saturday morning standing on Franklin Street in the muggy sunshine with a handful of leaflets, urging patrons to take their business elsewhere.

An observer was parked half a block away in front of a used-car place. This wasn't the busiest section of town, and the traffic that passed was usually in a hurry, on its way elsewhere. I liked that. Cars zipping along meant that their drivers were not bent on harassing a picket on the street. Nobody would call me names or throw things out the window.

I placed myself right on the steps, not so close that it would seem that I was blocking the entrance, but close enough so that I wouldn't have to walk far to hand a leaflet to someone who was about to climb the steps to the front door.

My partner this morning was David, a black UNC student. He was standing in the narrow grassy patch between the side door and the street, but he didn't have as much business as I did, for no blacks were going into the Dairy Bar.

I looked around at him occasionally—to see how he was doing, I told myself at first; but later I was honest and admitted to myself that it was also reassuring to see him there.

138

David was frail looking, though he was a little above average height. He was quiet and accommodating, and I liked him; I smiled watching him walk. He had been born and raised in one of the larger cities in the state.

At the main street entrance most of the whites looked the other way when I proffered the leaflet; some looked mean, but not really threatening; a few smiled at me. Mainly, though, it was a slow morning. Then my eye caught a green pickup truck parking on the side street.

Out of the truck emerged a red-haired giant: big shoulders, paunch, flushed, angry face. He was rapidly approaching the side entrance. David was rapidly approaching him. Which one would get to the door first? Dare David extend a leaflet to this man who was so obviously hostile? I held my breath. What was going to happen?

They met right at the side door. David held out a leaflet. I fully expected David to hit the sidewalk, a victim of the red man's blows. I strained to hear, but couldn't. My heart's pounding drove out the sounds. The two figures froze: David with pamphlet extended; the red man in a state just short of a physical attack.

I looked up and down Franklin Street. Not a car was in sight. The observer's car seemed a whole mile away, barely visible, and I couldn't call, though I wanted to. What would happen if the man hurt David? Should I go in the Dairy Bar and call the police? Would the patrons attack me? Where was the observer? But the observer could only see in her rear-view mirror. David was on the side. She couldn't see him. What should I do? I looked again. Nobody approached on foot. Nobody came out. Nothing in that whole town was moving. Everything was stopped.

David was going to get hurt.

I looked again and the frieze had broken. The side door swung violently open and the red-haired man entered the Dairy Bar. David, undismayed, started down the walk, and we met at the corner.

"What did he say, David?" I asked.

David answered, "He said, 'Boy, take that piece of paper and ram it . . .' " I tried not to hear as David relentlessly finished the man's statement, but I had to laugh in spite of myself.

The rest of our shift was uneventful.

11

In the spring, while it was still chilly, James Baldwin came to Durham. He was to speak in a white-owned bookstore in Durham and at North Carolina College.

James Baldwin was little, like a child, with big brothers and sisters following in his wake. He was black; they were white. It was a cold day, but he had on no topcoat. Those following in his wake did also. There was a muddy-blond young man with an enormous head of hair, cut in a bowl shape. He had on a brown jacket with a fleece lining. The collar was all heavy fleece. I looked curiously at him, for he looked so young to be a photographer for *Life* magazine, on assignment to cover America's hottest writer. The other photographers with him all looked alike. One, a woman, had on pants and looked and acted just like the rest. They were New Yorkers, that was easy enough to see. They had an air of imperviousness, as though they weren't really a part of the scene in the bookstore—they were just travelers moving through time on their way to a distant and far more important destination.

New Yorkers always gave me that impression, as if they were people from some far-off planet who inhabited earthling bodies but spoke a different language, had different customs and ways, and were indifferent to small-town talk. I envied them. To be able to wake up in the morning and not care what the neighbors thought—to live one day without being observed and commented on—must be heaven. Since I was a child, I had felt the eyes of people around me and had heard the unspoken comments.

So, the visitors from the city interested me. They were taking pictures with what seemed to be an invisible light. I once caught a narrow quick flicker of blue. There was no huge silver bulb going off in a blinding flash—just one flicker, and that was all.

But it was the writer that I had come to the bookstore to see. He was, of course, more than a writer, for he was black like me and had made himself the spokesman for the dreams of millions of blacks, including me. And he had a lot of glamour about him. I had heard Langston Hughes speak at the University of North Carolina at Chapel Hill a year or two earlier, and had even chatted with him at the reception; a brown, rotund man, genteel, he looked perfectly at home in that academic setting. I could easily have imagined him teaching an English course. But James Baldwin was something else again. He had an air of the big, big city. He had on short boots, and this was at least half a decade or more before boots for men became commonplace.

I was fascinated by the boots. They were gray suede that came up over the ankle and fastened with a silver clasp on the side. I wondered were they the latest fashion in New York, or Paris, or the world. Baldwin had on pants of some indefinable color, sort of a wine-like brown, and a plain jacket, also of a subdued color. Whatever his private life, the image that he projected that day was definitely low key.

I was staring at him intently, but not in a personal way. He was a real live author, and it was as though he were not really a person. I had read an interview in which Baldwin said that his father had once remarked that he was the ugliest child he had ever seen. I admired someone who could speak of his secret pain so frankly. It was so different from the way I had disciplined myself—to deny the hurts, suppress the pain, put a smooth, laughing face on everything. For me, to admit hurt was a sign of defeat. So no matter how hard the people around me struck, or how low, my habit was to laugh and pretend it didn't hurt.

Baldwin had an adult's head on a child's body. The body

was so tiny it was almost nonexistent. His eyes bulged, reptilian fashion, but that was not unusual to me. Protruding eyes were a feature in my family, on both my mother's and my father's sides. (It was said that protruding eyes were a feature of those who were slightly "off," meaning those who were stone crazy but hadn't done enough to warrant being sent to a mental institution.) Besides, my eyes protruded too.

So Baldwin looked like a rather friendly survivor of the age of giant reptiles. In movies I had seen, the giant reptiles loomed large over the people trying to escape from their stare. They would rear up and look around, and people, especially the heroine, would flee. Often the reptile would bite off tree tops, looking for the victim, who had had the good sense to take refuge in a cave. Evidently Baldwin was able to send a number of people flying by staring at them with that reptilian stare. But when it rested on me, I was unfazed; I stared right back at him.

The bookstore had been arranged like a church, with a few chairs on each side and the bulk of them turned to face the front. Baldwin was not in the pulpit section, but rather on the floor, in the middle, between the Amen Corners, sort of where the secretary sat in Sunday school. It was a small store and it was packed—mainly with students from North Carolina College and students and faculty from Duke and Chapel Hill.

Baldwin and I stared at each other for what seemed to be forever. I was so glad to see this world-famous writer and so mesmerized by him that I couldn't look away. He, on his part, eventually decided that I was not the enemy, and he smiled a smile that went clear across his face and embraced the whole room.

Damon and Pythias were there too. Of course those were not their real names, but what I called them, for I often saw them together at various meetings. They were what we used to call "dead buddies," meaning extraordinarily close. They had similar physiques—young, sturdy, healthy—but other than that, they couldn't have been more different. Damon was the son of an affluent white family; Pythias came from a black family near the poverty level.

Damon had brown hair, worn very full in the front, like President Kennedy's. He had big teeth and full lips; his mouth kept him for being really handsome. He and Pythias were both about the same height and weight, but Damon was sturdy, while Pythias tended to be rounded, a little soft. Pythias wore his hair cut close, and he had rather ordinary features; in fact he had no striking features at all. But his dedication to integration was total, and he worked untiringly for it. The civil rights movement had brought the two of them together; Damon had dropped out of UNC to help, and Pythias had dropped out of North Carolina College. On the surface these choices might seem to be the same, but they weren't. For if Damon decided to give it all up and return to school, he had a family, firmly situated in the Establishment, who could back him up. But for Pythias, going to college had been a very lucky chance, and he might not get another. But he didn't see it that way; the movement was the most important thing to him at the moment. I admired his courage. Already a different mentality was invading the consciousness of the black community.

I recognized Ed Wilson seated there in the bookshop; he was an artist, black, and a great admirer of James Baldwin. He was also the one intellectual contact that I had in Durham—he had many interests, read quite a lot, and loved to talk about his reading. And that was what I loved most in the world and needed most—talk. A talented man, Ed felt stifled at North Carolina College, and later, when white universities started recruiting black professors, Ed fled Durham.

Baldwin talked, and then there were questions. I had a question. I was so proud that I had read all of his writings, yet I had questioned some of his statements and asked him now about one of them. He said, "Yes, I see what you mean," and went on to describe what his state of mind had been when he wrote that. But I didn't hear what he said after "I see what you mean." He was a famous writer, respected at that time among the world's intellectuals. I had been scared to open my mouth. Yet not only had he been polite to me, he had also carefully pondered my question and given me a considered response. I had expected to be humiliated, as I so often was in the black community when I tried to discuss intellectual matters; yet he, who had been all over the world, had looked right at me, thought about my question, and given a serious response.

That evening he gave a second talk, and I went to hear him again. I knew how to beat the crowd, for I liked to arrive before everybody else. Then I could look over the whole auditorium, often wandering up and down the aisles, getting a feel of the place. Surroundings—the color of the seats, the draperies at the windows, or the lack of them, the runners in the aisles, whether they were worn rubber or faded red carpeting, the chairs and their arrangements—all had an effect on me. I used to say to myself, "I may never, ever in my life come into this auditorium again. How does it look? Could I paint it from memory? Suppose all the architects in the world were dead, could I design this building?"

In fact, one of my frequent fantasies was that all the people on the earth suddenly died, except me. And I found myself among the succeeding generation, who had no books, no pictures, no machines, no knowledge of what life had been like. Could I design the telephone? Electric lights? Could I describe an airplane and how it worked? Look at all the knowledge that I didn't have and had given up hoping that I would ever have. I used to think that I would like to go to school and take a major in every subject in the curriculum until I knew all about it. Finally admitting that this was impossible, I next tried to read a book on every subject. This, too, became too much.

But still the fantasies persisted. Suppose I were the only survivor of this civilization—what knowledge could I pass on to the next?

I didn't have time to do much fantasizing this evening. The auditorium was almost full when I got there, even though it was nearly an hour before Baldwin was to speak. I had to scramble to find myself a seat. Students were pushing to get seats, in a good-natured way. Anticipation was high. Most of the black college community had turned out, as well as a good number of white professors from Duke.

Baldwin read material that had been published in a much-discussed article in *The New Yorker*. Though the words were familiar, the way they were spoken was not. Written, they had been very interesting, but coming from the mouth of that little man with the stick legs and the big head, they were a mighty voice summoned up from the deep, a voice sounding down throughout the ages. The voice rolled on and filled up the auditorium, which was not an auditorium any longer. It was a deep, rounded chamber by a dark sea, and a message was pounding in on the surf, and the message told of truth, and it warned of despair. Caught up in the words and their message, which was the same as the words and yet somehow different, I lost track of space and time. I let go and listened to the surf pound up on the shore, again and again, now rising, now falling, but steadily continuing.

Traveler in distant lands though he was, Baldwin had mastered and had never forgotten the idiom of the black church. He had learned how to pick you up and set you down just where he wanted to. I wondered what it must be like to have power like that.

I was so washed away in the ocean that when it was over I listened but did not hear the questions. The auditorium, which had been filled with a mighty voice, was now filled with ordinary people using ordinary voices to ask questions, and try as I could, I could not understand ordinary voices that night.

What was Baldwin's secret? How had he come from such a long way, while others equally talented, or more so, had not? It seemed to me that he had acted in a nontraditional way. Maybe his personal agony had forced him out, but once he was out, he had a type of freedom that most people never know.

Perhaps that was what I should do—use my outsider status to walk around, not looking in on the world closed to me, but discovering the one outside. Perhaps that was the way. Explore the limits of whatever situation you find yourself in.

Could I do it? It would be hard for me to try. For I was Cancer in all respects: home-loving, centered on the family; reluctant to leave the familiar; desperate for a sense of community with my family, my group; failing in my attempts, but never ceasing to try. If I set out deliberately to explore possibilities, might I not get so far away that I'd never come back? And what about home and family and community and group? They were my sources of strength. If I got too far from them, I would lose the powerhouse, the energizer that had been supplying me with current for a long time. Or could it be that the energizer was internal, within myself, and that if I broke loose from family and community and group, I would be even more dynamic?

Two days later, when the *Carolina Times*, the black weekly, appeared, my picture was on the front page. There I stood in a greatcoat with a fur collar and a hat with wool petals next to James Baldwin, laughing at something he had said.

I was not even aware that my picture had been taken. But I silently thanked the photographer.

When the weather grew warmer in the late spring, Malcolm X came to Durham. I had never heard of Malcolm X until *Playboy* did an interview with him. I was stunned by his articulateness and the strength with which he presented his views. I was dismayed, however, when on the day he was to speak, or rather debate a local black leader, Floyd McKissick, I heard on the TV news that the city of Durham had refused to allow the meeting to take place as planned in the W. D. Hill Recreation Center and that it had been called off. I thought about it for a while, then called Mr. McKissick's office. His secretary told me that the meeting hadn't been called off, even though the meeting place had been canceled, and that Mr. McKissick was out of the office at the moment trying to find a place to hold

146

the meeting. I had the presence of mind to ask if Malcolm X was there. He was and he would speak to me as soon as his present caller hung up.

Thus it was Malcolm X himself who told me that the meeting would be at the union hall on Pine Street. I promised to be there.

Malcolm X had known the worst of the American system at first hand. His father had been so harassed by the Ku Klux Klan that the family had had to flee Nebraska. In a large Northern city, his father had died under mysterious circumstances. Malcolm X himself had grown to manhood in Detroit, one of America's great cities, and had taken to the streets at an early age. There he had mastered all the vices of the city and had become a criminal and eventually a convict. Converting to a U.S. black version of an Eastern religion in prison, he had again demonstrated his superior capability of mind and his natural leadership ability by quickly rising to the top in his sect's hierarchy, a sect that had branches all over the country. One of his jobs was to visit each branch, and that was what had brought him to Durham. Since he believed at that time that the white man was evil and that total separation from him was the best and only solution to the conflict of the races in the United States, he naturally had become a controversial figure among the civil rights activists, who were working very hard to have blacks integrated into the larger white community. Thus, he was to debate one of the local civil rights leaders. "Integration vs. Separation" was the subject of their debate.

Pine Street was dark, with artificial lighting. It looked like the lighting on residential streets, not a business area. For indeed it was a mixed business and residential area.

Though the street was lighted, it was dim and crowded. People who lived in the neighborhood parked their cars on the street, thus narrowing it even further. Sometimes it was necessary to drive over the center line just to keep moving.

Here, among old houses of black Durham's past glory, amid falling-down houses whose landlords wouldn't make any further repairs because they knew that urban renewal was going to take them all away anyhow, and a dozen little candy and sandwich shops that catered to the school children at Whitted School on the hill, stood the labor temple. Situated over a garage that was poorly kept up, it was the dingiest building in a street full of dingy buildings.

I was halfway afraid to go in. Some cabs were parked in front, and some men who must have been the drivers were standing around. I was afraid to go up to them and ask if this was the place; there was no sign. I looked casually around and tried to see where others were going. Two young men took to the stairs, and I knew that this must be the place. I went up the dusty steps, past the unpainted walls, into a small room with neatly arranged seats.

I was scared. Suppose hostile forces came to storm the meeting? We were upstairs, with the only exit a narrow stairway. We couldn't all possibly get out that way, and even if we could, the hostile forces could just stand at the foot of the stairs and pick us off one by one. Or they could simply set fire to the place and burn us all up. Thinking such thoughts as I looked for a seat, I failed to notice the other people there until I looked around and decided on the best course of exit. I had been in enough places where trouble might break out—black night clubs, for example—so that I automatically searched for the exit. Resigned to the fact that there was no good one, that I would have to take my chances along with the rest, I looked at my fellow early arrivals.

I was somewhat startled to see so many whites. But they were all seated on the right—none on the left. Then I noticed the ushers; they were very definitely steering blacks to the left side of the room and the whites to the right. They were practicing what they preached—segregation of the races. I looked in my own section. There were very interesting-looking blacks there, from different class and educational lines. Such was the power of Malcolm X that everybody wanted to hear him. The whites all looked professorial, probably from the neighboring white universities. I saw a man among them who looked out of place. Turning away, I looked toward the front, which was arranged like the Amen Corner, with benches facing each other instead of the front.

The civil rights movement was well represented at the debate and well integrated. They were there to cheer their leader and boo his opponent. For they were for integration and against separatism.

Among them, and very active and jolly, were Damon and Pythias. They were rather noisy, waving cheerfully to all their compatriots and supporters as they came through the narrow door. Pythias, I knew, had had an unbelievable experience a few nights earlier. While lying on the ground in front of a restaurant-motel during a sit-in outside Chapel Hill, he was urinated on by the white manager's wife.

Among the newcomers was a tall, very slender man. He took a seat on the platform and sat alone for a few minutes. It was not until I saw one of the students go up and start talking to the slender, light-skinned man that I realized that he was Malcolm X. He was on time and was unaccompanied at the moment. I recognized a compatriot spirit. He liked to get to places early and check them out beforehand, too. I went up to speak to him.

"Malcolm X," I said. "I called you earlier this evening."

The eyes looked dead at me and the voice said, "Yes, I know."

I was mortified. How did he know? Yet I had no doubt that he indeed *did know*. I supposed that it was my voice.

"Will there be time to talk after the meeting?" I asked. He nodded yes, and then turned to others who were standing waiting to talk to him. Men at the top always seem to have time to talk to anyone who wants to talk to them. Not only do they have the time, but also they seem to feel a need to do so. It must keep them in touch with the feel of things, and it probably explains how they got to the top in the first place and how they maintain their positions once they get there.

Malcolm X was the visitor, and he spoke first. Where was the quiet, slender man who had spoken to me just moments ago? He had disappeared and in his place was a moving shaft of light. It moved and moved and blinded me so that it filled the whole room and I could see nothing else. Other people faded away, seats, surroundings, everything. Just that moving long vertical light existed for me.

It was a mesmerizing experience. The speaker for integration, Floyd McKissick, who later would head CORE, couldn't equal Malcolm X and didn't try.

Then it was over: the speeches, the questions and answers, the charges and countercharges.

"Out of the way for Brother X! Out of the way for Brother X!"

Malcolm X's dark-suited functionaries were busily clearing a path. They had seen too many newscasts showing the rapid exit of the President of the United States following a press conference. Malcolm X had spoken to the crowd, and now he was moving on.

I stood to the side. I had wandered to the exit after I found him greatly occupied with the university types. Now I wondered if he had forgotten all about me. So when the dark-suited men came demanding that the aisle be made clear, I didn't know whether to stand to the side or not.

But he had told me that he would talk to me, and unless he distinctly told me no, I would assume that he meant yes.

Scared to death, both of a rebuff and of him, I nevertheless fell into step behind him, expecting momentarily to be tapped on the shoulder and requested to leave.

But nothing happened, and I soon found myself on the street standing beside him while the dark-suited men stood around. He motioned me into the car.

The car was so finely tuned that I didn't hear it when it took off. It was dark, and Malcolm X was silent. I said nothing, for I was overcome by my own audacity. When he did speak, he said, "That boy with the Bible!" and I realized that for all his bravura he was a sensitive man and had been offended when a black man had risen with his Bible and said, "Malcolm X, you're leading the people wrong," then launched into an attack against him.

We stopped at the College Inn. The light was dim on the outside of the building, like the light bulb in a living room, not like the large fixtures on a public establishment. But inside the lighting was fine.

The Inn was one long room, narrow, just wide enough for the row of booths lining the wall and a walkway between the booths and the counter stools. But the music was nice and the people well-dressed and happy. The crowd here was mainly college and young professional. There was a pleasant murmuring when Malcolm X walked in. Those who recognized him looked with at him with interest. Those who didn't continued to drink their Cokes or beer and talk to their friends.

Nina Simone was singing on a record, saying how nobody knows you when you're down and out, and if she ever got her hands on a dollar again, she'd hold it till the eagle screamed.

I thought that Malcolm X would have some caustic comments to make about the college-educated crowd or the pleasant atmosphere of the Inn. I thought that he would have preferred the company of sweat-stained, hard-working laborers or the ascetic environment of his own sect. But I was wrong. He obviously liked the place—something about the atmosphere pleased him.

I said little. Again he surprised me by commenting, "Some people hate us." He didn't seem to understand that. I murmured something, always conscious of his two dark protectors with their unsmiling faces directly across the table from us. We commented on movement events, and he surprised me by listening very attentively to what I had to say. That was the strange thing I was finding out about the people who were passing through Durham. They listened to me attentively, as if they found what I had to say interesting. While in Wildwood, my home, I had long ago ceased trying to make people understand, and at North Carolina College I had the impression that if I wanted to stay there any length of time I had better keep my mouth shut. It was so unexpected that I would get a chance to talk to Malcolm X that I came unprepared with a set of questions. I suppose that's why he seemed to relax after a while and gave me his address and told me to write to him. I was not an enemy; I didn't have an ax to grind; I didn't have a point of view to promote. I wanted to *know*. Then he said good-bye and the three of them were gone, he and his two bodyguards.

Yet for all my hero worship, I couldn't help noting and filing away the fact that when Malcolm X paid for the orange juice he had ordered for us, he paid off under the table. The years of criminality had left him with one gesture that he couldn't eradicate. In spite of myself I had noticed this, and made the simultaneous observation that a man's habits become so ingrained that even if his life changes, some of his habits do not.

Also, I was not unaware that my personal response to Malcolm X had probably affected to some extent my intense response to his message. If I had heard the message from a less attractive, less charismatic man, I wonder if my response would have been so immediate. I was attracted to the philosophy of black nationalism, but not to its religious arm, for I felt unable to accept the role that the sect had assigned to women. I suppose that what it boils down to is that I never liked being told what to do, what to think, how to act. My question was always, "Why?" And I frequently wouldn't do whatever it was because someone was telling me what to do.

Later, in the late 1960s when I was talking about Malcolm X to one of my brother Jesse's many girlfriends, a woman who I am convinced was once a street prostitute in New York City, she told me that she knew "Red" (Malcolm X's nickname) well; in fact, she had once been his girlfriend. I wanted to know what kind of lover he was. She gave him all plusses. In fact, she went on, they were still friends, and once she had met him in Harlem after he became a minister and he had sat and talked with her for a while. He said to her, "You know, Sister, you ought to take care of yourself. Don't be like Betty.

You know what happened to her." It seems that Betty's "man" killed her, then cut away her genitals and put them in the freezer. That way no other man could ever have her again.

I was still curious about Malcolm X, and I asked her what sort of person was he really like. And she said, "He was a nice person, but he always wanted me to—" and then she broke off and changed the subject. But she didn't have to finish the story, for I knew what the ending was: she was going to say that he always wanted her to go out with men and give him the money. I wondered if that was what they broke up about.

James Baldwin and Malcolm X had both had an impact on me long before I met them, primarily because their lives were outside the conventional mode and each man, in his own way, had turned his "outsideness" into something that had meaning. If Malcolm X and James Baldwin did not themselves believe in the images that they had created, or if the cognoscenti did not, still there were large numbers of people who did—the personas that they had created had meaning for a lot of people. Black amorphous personalities seeking to form firm, sharply outlined personalities had in the 1960s what they had not had in American life for many decades: a number of recognizable, acceptable patterns or life-styles to choose among. Not only were there these two men, but also Dr. Martin Luther King, Jr., the SNCC people, the CORE people, the NAACPers, and others, some of whom received only brief, local renown before they faded from memory with the passing of the sixties. Others never received any recognition at all. Even more romantic personas blossomed in the late 1960s with the reemergence of black nationalism and the Black Panthers and others like them. They were much more flamboyant, dashing, and charismatic than the personalities of the early sixties, and that, I feel, may be one reason why the black nationalists pushed the early civil righters into the shadows: the personalities that they outlined day by day in the media, particularly television, were so much more sharply outlined and romantic that those with amorphous personalities, trying to find a *self*, turned to them.

153

Part
FOUR

12

After serving as a temporary replacement at NCC, I had been given an appointment as an instructor, and had held that post for several years. Then the administration introduced what they called a rating system. This was based on a list of about ten items, ranging from community involvement to committee work to attitude, under each of which were the legends "Excellent," "Good," "Fair," and "Poor." The chairman of the department, Carroll Light, had the sole prerogative of rating each member as he saw fit. Rumor had it that the system originated with the dean of the graduate school.

The purpose of the system was soon clear, and rumors sped through the faculty about who had received the high ratings and who had received the low ones. It was rumored that the highest rating in my department was given to a woman who belonged to the same bridge club as the president's wife. The man who had the longest list of publications in my department, who had previously served as chairman of the department for more than thirty years, received one of the lowest ratings; the administration had hated him for a long time because he didn't think the administrators were very bright and had let them know it. Everybody was upset. Some cried, others cursed, but few did anything else.

I should not have been surprised at my rating of 71 percent, but I was very, very hurt. Grades had meant so much to me all my life because that was the one area where I had had some success, and to be rated that way, without even being consulted, was a bitter thing to me.

I went to see the president about the matter, and he told me that there was an appeals board that I should apply to. I hadn't even known that, for nothing had been said about appealing. I also got the distinct impression from him that there was little hope in doing so, but as I sat there, black and glowering (although technically he was black, his skin was as clear and white as parchment), telling him how wrong all this was, he seemed to shift slightly in his attitude; again he said to see the appeals board. The president appointed the appeals board.

I went, along with some others from various departments on the campus. One was a woman who had a doctorate. I was surprised to see her, for she was one of *them*—light-skinned, silver-haired, and overbearing. But it seems that once, so she said, she had rebuffed the president's advances, and besides, he was now fascinated with a younger version of herself in her department—and so he was taking this opportunity to let her know where she stood with him.

The appeals board was composed of several people, one of whom was an elderly man from the history department. The others were a younger man who had presidential ambitions and affected a grave and pompous manner, and another member of the administration, who had once told his psychology class that he didn't believe there was such a thing as love—that all he wanted to do in the sex act was raise a holler and that was enough for him.

This was the impartial committee chosen to hear appeals.

About the kindest suggestion that was made to me came from the elderly man: he suggested that I go back to school and work on my doctorate. I thought that he was being mean, for he knew and I knew that very few of the faculty at NCC had doctorates and that many of those teaching with master's degrees hadn't been back to school in many years; to force me to meet a requirement that others did not have to meet was unfair. But now I sometimes think that he was telling me in his own way that the system was unfair and the best way to beat it was to get a doctorate. He probably told me this because he was retiring soon himself. But then again, I think, he was always part of the system, and perhaps they employed him to give that message to everybody, utilizing his gray hair and years.

I don't know why I didn't resign at the end of the term—just plain inertia, I guess. That was part of it. But another and more important factor, perhaps, was that I knew that if I resigned I would have to leave Durham, leave home, and that was a thought I never let myself think. For somehow I couldn't leave home, go away from all that was familiar. Besides, how would I get along? I had been told and I felt that I was unable to cope in the everyday world, that disaster awaited me the moment I took my head out of a book, for I had no common sense, nothing with which to face the real world. And I still operated on such a notion, even though I had my own apartment—largely unfurnished, it's true, but mine nevertheless—and I was managing, not as well as I should, but still managing. However, in some way I came to believe that the main reason that I didn't go under immediately was the fact that I was so close to home, where I could still receive parental advice—negative stroking, as it were—and I was fearful of what would happen to me without it.

So I hesitated and waited, half hoping that my appearance before the appeals committee would count for something. The contracts and salary raises would be awarded in the late summer. Then I would see.

Summer came and I decided to go to summer school again at Chapel Hill. I didn't have a special reason; it was just that I enjoyed learning new things, and school was the only place where I really felt at home. I had a master's degree and the thought of getting another, more advanced degree had never crossed my mind seriously. Yet I went.

In mid-August, notice of pay raises were sent out. I had received a two-hundred-dollar-per-year raise. I promptly tried to resign, but I soon received a letter from the president telling me that I couldn't, for there were less than thirty days before the start of the new term and I hadn't given thirty days' notice. I wrote back and asked for a leave of absence so that I could go to graduate school and get further training in order to qualify for a promotion. The leave was granted, but for the second semester. Thus, I had to remain at the college another semester.

It was a bad time. I don't remember what I taught or how I taught, for I just wanted to get away. The pain of staying when it was clear that I wasn't wanted and the refusal of the authorities to let me go when I wanted to go had gotten to me.

One day in the early fall, I noticed one of my students, Louisa, sleeping at her desk. That was unusual for her; a chunky brown girl with translucent skin, she was always bright and cheerful. I asked her about it after class and she told me that she hadn't eaten in several days. I invited her home for supper. Over the meal she told me that she didn't have anywhere to stay, that she was managing by sleeping in the dormitory, first this one's, now that one's bed, because her mother in eastern North Carolina had sent her up to Durham with just tuition money. She had had a job in the dining hall to pay for her board and to get a room off campus, but she had been fired, she said, for giving extra-large portions when the students asked for them. I told her she could stay with me and that she could eat when I ate; her only job would be to keep the apartment swept and the dishes washed; there was little furniture to see after. So she moved in, sleeping on the sofa bed in the sitting room. She was a good companion, a cheerful girl who nearly ate me out of house and home, and who promptly dropped the silver down the sink so that I had to call the plumber. But she laughed easily, and I was glad to have someone in the house, for it made me feel less lonely.

But mainly I waited. I didn't know for what. Life wasn't supposed to turn out the way it had; life was supposed to have meaning. Mine didn't seem to have any, therefore I thought something was very wrong with it. What it was I didn't know and perhaps never would know, but something was wrong.

In November 1963, someone shot the President. A student in my afternoon class looked out of our upper-floor classroom and said, "Miss Mebane, they just lowered the flag. The President is dead."

I sat and watched the television set. Two of the young women students in one of my classes went to Washington and stood all night in line to pass the bier.

January 1964 was a gray month, not particularly cold, but heavy and very hard, like metal. I viewed it as the end for me. To a casual observer I guess it would have seemed to be the start of something. I was breaking up housekeeping, giving up my apartment on Fayetteville Street, returning to my mother's house. I would go to graduate school at Chapel Hill to work for a doctorate in English. No one in my immediate family had even been to college, and few of my first-cousin peers had finished high school. And I had a bachelor's degree and a master's degree and I was going to do even further study. That would have been the sensible way to look at it, I guess, but I seemed, instead, to see it as a failure.

I said good-bye to my young friend, Louisa, who had been a lively spot in the gloom, but here, too, I felt despondent. For Louisa, with all her desire and truly diligent work, was unsuited for academic work. This was sad, for Louisa wanted more than anything in the world to get a college education. She was a farm girl from eastern North Carolina, from a large family, none of whom had gone to college. Somehow she had gotten it into her mind that she would go, though she was ineligible for a scholarship. After losing her job in the dining hall, she was left with literally nothing. She told me of several other girls in similar situations, living in Durham while they went to college and having very little means to do so. She told me about one of her friends who had been going with a factory worker who had given her clothes and money. She grew tired of him and withdrew. One day he caught up with her, right on Fayetteville Street, and insisted that she give him back every piece of clothing that he had given her: first the coat, then the sweater, then the skirt. At that, she ran and he let her go.

I wished so much that Louisa could realize her dreams. I thought of the strangeness of human life: Here was a young woman who would have worked long hours over her books, who would have undergone any type of deprivation, who would have done any type of work, just to get a college degree. But she was not suited for it. Whereas I had met other young women, her peers, some of whom were very talented and could have succeeded at almost anything they tried, yet they were frequently uncaring and seldom gave their full effort to anything. Louisa, if she had had a small portion of their potential, would have used it to become a success.

During my period of graduate study at Chapel Hill I would receive several grants from various sources: the Southern Fellowships Fund in Atlanta, Georgia; the Woodrow Wilson Career Teaching Fellowship from the Department of English at the University of North Carolina; dissertation year grants from the Southern Fellowships Fund. I also received several loans from the University, all of which were repaid.

13

Sleep, which had been gradually slipping away from me, became a fugitive, appearing ever so briefly and unexpectedly now and then. Without sleep, I thought all the time. My mind turned over and over and over. The motor never stopped running. When I got up in the morning I was tired, for the motor had run all night, I had felt it running even in my dozing, and I had no relief. The search for sleep occupied me for nearly seven years. I tried everything. My therapist gave me Librium, and while it tranquilized me, it didn't make me sleep. I went to the student infirmary and they gave me other types of medication, but they did no good.

I went to Duke Medical Center and pleaded for sleep, just a few nights, and was given a prescription for capsules about the length of a fingernail filled with a heavy red liquid; they were "knockout drops." And they would do just that. I would wait for sleep until two in the morning, and if it didn't come by then I would get up and take a red capsule. Before I put my head on the pillow, a heavy hammer would hit me on the head and knock me out. And I would get three or four hours' sleep. I was scared of those capsules, for I had been told that two could be fatal, and I was afraid that sometime I might in my sleep take an additional one and it would be all over for me. So I hid them, leaving just one where I could get to it quickly, putting the bottle where it would surely be hard to get to if I should walk in my sleep.

I took those red capsules, but still I wanted something else, something a little safer than knockout drops. So I devised a dose of two aspirin and a Librium capsule. It left me groggy and fatigued the next day, but I could get a type of sleep. This I was not afraid of, though several times a week I needed the deep sleep that the knockout drops gave me. From 1964 to 1971 I seldom knew a night of natural sleep.

In February, by the time I had enrolled and gotten settled in at the University, I knew that something was seriously wrong. For I found that I could not concentrate. I would pick up a book and start to read and, whereas for most of my life I could get absorbed in almost any book, whether for information or for pleasure, and not look up for twenty or thirty minutes or sometimes even an hour, I now found it difficult to follow the writing for as much as a page. I would start reading in the library, but then from somewhere stray thoughts would come and take control, so insidiously that before I knew it I would find myself on a tangent, thinking thoughts far away from the book or from the time and place I was in. What in the world! I would think, chiding myself for a lack of discipline. Then I would start over. Finally I managed to read one page at a time; I would reward myself each time by getting up and stretching or walking up and down a little in my carrel or taking down a current periodical and reading something light. For that was the curious thing—I could read current magazines with no trouble. Then I would go back to my reading, stopping again after each page. It was laborious work, but by spending long hours in my carrel every day, including Saturday and Sunday, I could keep up, and that was the important thing: not to fail.

I was terrified, for I had never had this trouble before. Finally I went to the reading clinic and was tested and put on a program designed to improve my reading speed. I stayed for about three weeks, but found that wasn't effective either.

Next, I noticed that in addition to finding stray thoughts taking over my mind in the middle of a page, I sometimes couldn't think at all. It was as though there were a radio and I heard static. Gradually the static took over, and I couldn't hear what I was reading. I knew despair. For who would help me? Though I still saw my therapist, I spent a good deal of time assuring him that I was all right and that things were working out just fine—when in reality I was in worse shape than I had ever been.

What was most frightening of all was that time disintegrated. It was as though time were a liquid in a bottle that suddenly broke, and it ran out, all over the place, without form, without pattern, without meaning. I tried to catch it and hold it and shape it into a meaningful pattern, but I couldn't. Sometimes I would get up in the morning and, after what seemed to be an interminable time, look at the clock, to discover that it was only nine or ten a.m. I didn't understand how this could be, for it seemed that I had lived a whole day.

During this period I realized how important time structures were. You get up and do certain things until lunch, then you do certain things after lunch, then you do certain things in the evening. You follow a routine four or five days a week; then on the weekend you do something different. I was without that structure. I had once been in time, but now I was out of time, while others around me were moving in it. And try as hard as I could, I couldn't seem to get back in time.

In January my car had given out. One day I tried to start it and it wouldn't go. It was a 1954 Chevrolet that I had bought secondhand in 1959. It was bad luck for my car to quit just as I was getting ready to leave a regular job, but to me it was just one of those things. I thought that I would get another one, again secondhand. Perhaps it would last me as long as the Chevy had, in which case I would be through graduate school and able to afford a new one. I read the ads carefully and found a likely one. I bought it with five hundred dollars that I had saved. Two weeks into the new term it, too, quit cold. I took it back and was told that it had a cracked motor—cost of repairs: three hundred dollars. I was so hurt that I just parked it in front of the door and walked away. They knew that the motor was cracked when they sold it to me, when they had a spanking brand-new coat of silver paint on it and all the fixtures inside gleamed. But I didn't have three hundred dollars more for repairs, so I was out of a car and out of my money. I moved into the dorm at Chapel Hill.

In looking back I see that incident as the start of a series of financial disasters that left me deeply in debt. For during the rest of the decade, I never was out of debt; indeed, sometimes I was barely able to meet my obligations. I couldn't seem to manage. There were others with fellowships who seemed to do all right, but I couldn't. I was always behind and incapable of managing my money—paying my bills on time and having some left over. I didn't know what the matter was, for I hadn't always been like that. Indeed, it was once my pride that promptly on payday I put checks in the mail to everybody I owed. I couldn't believe that I was the same person I had been then.

I had heard of faith healers, for they were a part of the landscape in the black South. In my neighborhood, the Holy church across the road from us had regularly—as part of their services—held prayer for the sick, the "laying on of hands." The neighbors' testimonies were full of references to cures of various ailments that had yielded to prayer. Now that I was sick and couldn't get well and had lost all faith in Western medicine, I decided to consult Mother Brown, a renowned faith healer in Durham who preached in a Holy and Sanctified church. She walked the streets day after day to spread her gospel, and sometimes in her home she gave advice and counsel to the weary, to those who like me, were tired and unable to find the way.

As I approached her cinder-block house on a cement walk in Braggtown, I saw meticulously tended flowers around the steps. I knocked and peeked through the curtained glass window. Inside, the sun fell on the floor, and I could see chairs and an old upright piano in the corner.

"Yes." A brown face was looking at me, smooth and unwrinkled, with clear level eyes.

She sounded just as she had on the telephone. Instead of answering, "Hello," she had answered, "Yes," which had put me off for a while.

"I'm the one who called you," I said.

"Come in, child," she said. She was wearing a spanking clean, long white dress, with a white scarf flowing from her head. Her face crinkled in a warm smile, her teeth gleaming, as she welcomed me to her house. It was a typical Southern black home. There were starched, crocheted pieces standing in convoluted majesty all around on flat surfaces. This was a form of popular art that was common in the region. Some of the pieces were at least a foot high. Women put sugar in the starch to make them stand up firmly. There were chairs full of fat pillows covered in fading chintz. I sat on the edge of the old-fashioned, three-pillow sofa, directly opposite a large brown wood-burning stove.

Directly over the stove was a picture of Jesus Christ dressed in crimson velvet with white gold scattered around his head. His gaze looked out over my head.

On the left was another old-fashioned, chintz-covered, three-pillow sofa, and over it was a picture of Jesus Christ praying on his knees. Without a moment's hesitation, I knew it was Jesus in his hour of trial, asking God to deliver the "bitter cup" from Him.

Over the piano on the right were two pictures thumbtacked to the wall: Jesus with a staff and sheep all around him and a photo of a brown young man in a khaki uniform with a peaked cap. The picture looked dated. What war was this? World War II? Korea? The picture didn't look old enough to be World War I. Was it her son? Did he die in the war? Was he wounded? Did her prayers help him? I wondered as I looked at him, smooth-faced and forever young—frozen in the photograph.

Directly in front of me, through an open door, I saw a huge, old-fashioned mahogany bed, with a heavy white coverlet with a raised beaded pattern. It looked all made up as if for a wedding—or to lay somebody out who was dead. Had someone died in that bed? Did people actually sleep there? Was it kept for show? How could Mother Brown afford such an expensive spread? But then I knew that "respectable" black folk always set good store in cleanliness and order in the "front room." I had sat in innumerable front rooms when I went to visit the parents of my eighth-graders when I taught in the public schools in Durham. The scene was usually the same: a starched, high, convoluted, crocheted piece in the center of an oval-shaped coffee table, sometimes with a glass covering, with old Kodak snapshots underneath—sepia photos of parents, frequently showing the man with his arm around the woman's neck: he with his hat on his head, often with a tooth missing; she with a gap between her teeth and straightened hair smoothed down on either side of a "part," or curled back in a pompadour or forward toward the front in a bang. There were also black-and-white wedding pictures; children with their Christmas presents; even an occasional nightclub scene, with a tax-paid whisky bottle and some beer cans on the table. The newer pictures were always easier to spot; they were in color and were often of children—sometimes taken in Germany or wherever the U.S. Army had sent the son of the family. Then sometimes the coffee table would be square, not oval, with a ruffled edge of wood standing up all around the edges. But always on it were crocheted pieces that stood up very high.

The other areas of the front room also looked the same. The chairs would be covered in chintz, faded from many washings, and on the walls, thumbtacked or in frames—family pictures and religious pictures, New Testament pictures. Not infrequently there was a piano in the room. The rest of the home may have been in disarray, but the front room was always immaculate.

So, I should not have been surprised at the quiet and order and cleanliness in Mother Brown's room.

"What is it, darling?" she asked.

"All I ever seem to have is bad luck. I think God has cursed me. People don't like me and I don't know why," I said without pause.

"Child, you don't know how well off you are," Mother Brown said. She expressed no surprise, shock, or dismay, but continued. "Now, darling, don't cry. Everything's going to be all right. God is able. He's got all power in his hands. Oh, if only people would come to God. He's able." Here she leaned back in her chair as if in pain, wondering why people didn't put their trust in God. "Child, don't you know God is able? He's able! He's able! Able to carry us through. If only people would know God. My God is able. He said He would be a help in the time of trouble. He said he would. He said he would be shelter in the time of a storm. He said He would. Oh, yes, He said He would. People ought to trust Him. Only trust in God. . . . I was down, but He raised me. He raised me! But He said that all power was in His hands. And He said that if you do it even to the least of my little ones, you do it to me. He can lift you up. I was down but He lifted me. I was at the place where I didn't know which way to go, but God rescued me. Oh, yes, He did. He's a rock in a weary land. A shelter in the time of a storm. He said, 'Know me, I your God am a jealous God.' People put everything before God. But, child, He's able. Only trust Him. He'll carry you through. Can't you trust Him?"

I looked up from crying and saw her rocking from side to side, her eyes closed, utter conviction on her face. On the inner lids of her closed eyes I imagined that she saw the whole history of our ethnic group and how we had come through, how we survived the middle passage—crossing in the heat, stench, and hunger of the slave ships. She saw the slave auctions and the hard-faced no-color men with eyes like agate, who later in our history looked at the camera near a black burnt body, eyes glittering. And God was able; we had survived.

She was saying what I wanted to hear: that God was able, that He cared for all of His children. But something inside resisted, still would not believe.

"But why doesn't He care for me? Why does He punish me all the time? I've tried all my life—I've tried to do what's right. I've worked in the church, I was secretary of the Sunday School; I played for the choir, I went to church; I never did anything but go to school, to church, to town, and to work, and what do I have for it? I don't have a husband; I can't seem to be able to hold on to my money. People criticize me all the time. Nobody appreciates what I'm doing; I'm an outcast."

"Child, what do you want to get married for? You know, I was married, but I wasn't happy. You know, one time that man came after me to kill me. They stopped him before he got to me." When she talked about her personal life her voice was higher, and human indignation was in it. But when she turned to talk of God, she closed her eyes and her voice sounded like a low-toned, rich-throated variation of the Catholic priest's chant.

I had stopped crying. She was holding my hands sandwich-fashion between hers, and I wanted somehow to acquire her faith, her certainty that God was good, that He was watching over all. I only knew that my days on this earth had been cursed, and I secretly believed that God was doing it. It was blasphemy, but I believed it. I couldn't help it. The litany went on.

"God loves you, honey," she said.

"But why does He punish me?"

"He singles out the ones He loves."

"But am I not going to ever have any good luck?" I wanted to believe but couldn't quite.

"God knows what's best for us. Take your cares to the Lord and leave them there. Sometimes He tries us to test us, and when He tests us we are strong. Look at Job, honey. Everything he lost was restored many times over." Mother Brown had utter conviction in her voice.

"But I hurt so bad inside—why are people so mean to me? I try all I can to make them like me. Why aren't they ever satisfied? Why do they criticize me all the time?"

"Honey, God is able. Yes, He is. If only folks would learn to take their burdens to the Lord and leave them there. He's able.

"Fast and pray," she continued. "Fast and pray. It gives you strength. Once I went seven days without eating or drinking. Wasn't no one in Durham but me strong enough to do that. And you can fast. I'll go with you sometimes."

We knelt together on the hard floor, and Mother Brown talked to God, intoning His name and occasionally interrupting with handclaps and exclamations of, "Yes, Lord!"

I left later, half hoping and half believing that God—through His intermediary, Mother Brown—would cease persecuting me and give me peace of mind.

It was just about this same time that I became acquainted with Mrs. Jackson. I had admired a hat a neighbor was wearing and was surprised when she told me that it was handmade; a black lady living in Durham named Mrs. Jackson had worked on that marvelous creation.

I went to see her, for I still attended church then and wore

170

hats on Sunday. Mrs. Jackson was of that indeterminate age between sixty and seventy: she could have been a little older, she could be a little younger, one couldn't tell. She was about five feet six and weighed about a hundred and forty pounds. She was quite shapely, with a well-defined waist, neat full hips, modest chest, and smooth full legs. It was easy to see that as a young and middle-aged woman, Mrs. Jackson must have had a stunning figure. She was evidently a "dresser" back then, too, for now she wore clothes from her wardrobe that had once been fashionable, from the days when she dressed in style. She always wore high-heeled shoes, saying that she had worn them so long that it hurt her to wear low heels. Her skin was a clear and unmarked brown, and she had a marvelous smile. Age had hurt her most by drawing down her features, for she had worked at night so much making hats and flowers by artificial light that her eyelids now had a permanent, rather severe droop that pulled her whole face down, especially the lines beside her nose, lower lip, and chin. She wore her grayish hair undyed.

Mrs. Jackson lived in a shambling house with false brick siding, at the end of a dirt street that branched off from Fayetteville Street, the leading street in black Durham. The street ran down to a little wood, and on the hill was a park. Sometimes I could hear the shouts of children coming from the playground when I went to visit her, and I visited her often, for to me she represented something that I believed existed and that I so desperately wanted to find. She was the "folk," the people, and she had survived. I believed there was some secret knowledge that had enabled black people to survive, and if I ever had it, I had lost it. During the sixties I tried to find it, mainly by talking to and questioning black folk.

Mrs. Jackson had lived a very interesting life. She had traveled with a gospel chorus all up and down the Atlantic seaboard, and they had done extensive touring in the South. I liked to listen to her stories of those days. After I got to know her better, she told me about other facets of her life. It seems that there once was a man in one town who became infatuated

with her when he heard her sing. And from then on, periodically he would catch up with the group on the road and attempt to see her after every concert, to declare his love for her.
She would listen but wouldn't encourage him. Then he would
give her a twenty-dollar bill, to show his regard for her. She
didn't know what to do with the money, for her husband
would be suspicious if she started spending money he hadn't
given her. She wore a cloth coat with a large fur collar, and
when her admirer gave her money, she would pin it under her
fur collar. And she wouldn't let anybody, especially her husband, help her on with her coat.

She didn't see any incongruity in singing gospel music in
churches night after night with twenty-dollar bills from a secret admirer pinned under the coat collar. I did. But I tried
hard to see life from her point of view. An admirer had given
her money. She accepted it. Times were hard for everybody,
and for black people most of all. Twenty dollars was quite a
bit of money in those days.

Once her touring days were over, Mrs. Jackson settled in
Durham. She sold flowers on Main Street, both fresh flowers
and beautiful handmade flowers. And she also sold hats.

Sometimes I talked to her of the pain in my life and the fact
that I couldn't relate to men. Mrs. Jackson couldn't understand
that at all. She had had three husbands and "more boyfriends
than you can mention." She just couldn't understand what
was wrong that I couldn't get a boyfriend.

"Boyfriend," as both of us came to realize, was just a code
word for sex. For I was locked into a most cruel dilemma: I
couldn't get a boyfriend but I was really quite "high-natured"
(passionate).

Once when Mrs. Jackson was reminiscing, she told me
about a trip to New York that she took with a Durham banker. I didn't ask any questions, but instead just let her talk. I
wondered who the man was. Was he old or young? I could
somehow picture him, graying and distinguished-looking,
stopping to speak to the shapely woman selling flowers on
Main Street; a few words, and an assignation was made. And

so they went away. I wanted to ask her how long they knew each other? How did it start? When did it end? But I didn't. I was struck rather by the fact that Mrs. Jackson was as matter-of-fact about that relationship as she had been about the twenty-dollar bills. She became young again as she told me about the good time she had had with him at Coney Island. Her only regret at the time was that she couldn't tell anybody about it; she had to be content with hugging herself and smiling in the dark whenever she thought about it.

I visited Mother Brown and Mrs. Jackson frequently, for there was something that I wanted from those women, some view of what life was really like. I saw two different women, about the same age, both black folk, but their responses to life had been totally different. Their views of right and wrong, of the best way to live, couldn't have been more far apart, I thought, if they lived on different planets.

"Miss Mildred" was a neighbor in Wildwood, about the same age as Mother Brown. She used to tell me, when I sat at her kitchen table in despair, "It isn't your time yet. Your time is coming." She always said it with absolute conviction in her voice.

14

I have a special tie to Chapel Hill, mainly, I suspect, because some people at the University respected my gifts, and that was a first for me. Like many others, once I went there I never really wanted to leave. I think a number of people come to the University escaping from the barrenness and lack of nurturing, if not downright hostility, of small towns and villages all over the South and nation. Once a little of the pressure of such places is relieved—even if for just a little while—one never really wants that pressure to settle in on him or her again. I suspect that that is why I clung to the University for

173

so long. For after I enrolled full-time in the spring of 1960, I never completely broke my ties with the University until the day I defended my dissertation in 1972. Before I started serious graduate study, I was always taking one course here and another there; I attended performances of the Carolina Playmakers and other events; I kept in touch with various people there, whether I was actually enrolled or not, on through the sixties. It was easier for me than most to stay in touch, for I lived only about twenty minutes away. Any flowering of my talent that occurred later started there.

In my lighter moments now, I sometimes joke that the only people I had in my life for a long time were (1) sickies, (2) exploiters, and (3) very bad people. These people gravitated toward me because they seemed to feel that I had more strength than they had, and more important, they sensed my lack of self-esteem and so felt better about themselves. One element in these relationships, however, made for a great deal of tension: for all their problems, these people thought that I was holding a much better hand than I thought I had.

I did have some dealings with constructive personalities, though, people who liked me and wanted to help. They had seen me peering out of the thick, clear plastic inverted bowl where I was trapped, and these constructive people would tap on the glass and beckon to me to come out. But although I saw them beckoning, I thought that there must be some mistake. Who? Me? A valuable person? *Me?* I was someone who had been told that I was odd, strange, curious, and couldn't do anything right. Indeed, I was going to wind up in Goldsboro (the mental institution for blacks in North Carolina). I stayed under the glass, therefore, feeling that if I went out people would soon enough discover their mistake and send me right back in again. And that would be doubly hard; for, having experienced some happiness, I would find it nightmarish to accept the bad again. Besides, how could I get out? I had walked around the circumference of the clear plastic bowl for years and had never seen an exit sign.

Jessie Rehder was a writer and a North Carolinian. She was white. She seemed to be in her mid-fifties and had brown hair, liberally mixed with gray, which she wore in sort of a short pageboy, all around her head. Her skin looked rather sallow, like that of the farm women you sometimes see in town on a Saturday after they've spent the week in the field or kitchen. Jessie always wore comfortable shoes and carried a briefcase. I was surprised when I was told that she headed the creative writing program at the University, for I had been so conditioned by my experiences at North Carolina College that I could scarcely picture a "head" dressed that way. At black colleges, women who played a certain role dressed the part. They were black college teachers, and that meant they had to dress up.

I had been one of the few women on the faculty at North Carolina College who didn't "dress." I knew that most women at the college dressed up to show others that, though they were black, they were not cooks or elevator operators. Now, here at the University of North Carolina, I discovered a re-spected woman who acted as if "outfits" were the furthest thing from her mind.

I was even more impressed when I learned that Jessie herself was a writer, for I looked up to writers: to be able to create a whole world and people it, bringing it to life, was magic. I thought that writing was a talent like playing the piano by ear; people who had the talent simply sat down and played a tune they had heard. They were gifted people. I had come from a background where musical talent was abundant but where literary talent seldom raised its head, or was quickly suppressed if it did. So it did not occur to me that one day I might be a writer. I felt that it just wasn't in my genes, though I often looked up from a book and secretly wished that I could write. I knew of Colette and had heard that she was part black; I'd even read some of her work in translation. But I knew she had a special genius, and I also knew that she had been born in France, a country that was not as repressive as the United States.

Sometimes I would go and stand in Jessie's door and talk. She always invited me to come in, but at first I'd have some excuse not to—I was on my way to class, I had to go to the library, I was going to lunch. I hung back, for my experience had taught me to proceed with care in trying to make human contacts. But one day, I don't remember how, I found myself seated in Jessie's office. Close up, she still looked like a country woman, which was natural, for she came from the eastern part of the state and still had the accent of the region. But she also had a direct way of speaking that both startled and interested me, for at that time I still used the circumlocutions commonly found among the folk in the South. It is a manner of talking in which no one says directly what he or she means, but talks in sort of right-angle lines; a person who understands that kind of talk will deduce the meaning from what isn't said as well as from what is said. I didn't know if that way of expressing oneself was confined to the black folk or was shared by both blacks and whites on the lower socioeconomic levels, for I seldom talked to whites until I went to the University, and naturally, the University tended to level many class distinctions. However, it is a way of speaking that is almost impossible to reproduce for someone who has not heard it, and though I used to understand it perfectly and practiced it a lot myself, I now find that I'm impatient when listening to others who still express themselves that way.

I gave a start of surprise the first day I heard Jessie "cuss." Something had gone wrong, and she said, "Damn." I sort of expected something to happen, like maybe part of the sky to fall, but it didn't. I didn't swear, for a black woman was immediately classified as low-class if not downright immoral if she used the so-called "cuss words." Words like "hell" and "damn" were, of course, blasphemous to churchgoers—they even frowned on such expressions as "My God." They called it "taking the Lord's name in vain." "Lord have mercy" was all right, though; they probably convinced themselves that they were uttering a prayer. College-exposed black women carefully excluded any cuss words from their vocabulary. So I never said a bad word, though at times I had thought of some far more terrible than "Damn"—that was my secret.

Secretly I envied Jessie's freedom to say what she wanted to say. One day, somehow, I managed to swear. Though I fully expected everyone to turn and look at me with scorn, no one seemed to notice, and though I expected God Himself personally to reach down from Heaven and strike me dead, He didn't. I don't know if it was Jessie's influence or not, but it represented a loosening that was part of the *zeitgeist* of the mid-sixties. One layer of the cocoon I was wrapped in was unwound. But I still had a thousand layers to go.

Jessie talked candidly to me about some of her career headaches. She once pointed out to me a man in the department who hadn't spoken to her the first ten years she was at the university. He was a full professor and a published scholar, while she was a writer without a doctorate, and a woman, and he didn't seem to think it was worth his while to pass the time of day with her. Although he had recently started to speak to her, Jessie was still mad at him. Jessie talked so straightforwardly with me that gradually I began to open up just a little to her and tell her things about my life.

On occasion she invited me to her home, and after hesitating for a long time, I decided to go. She lived in a modest house in Chapel Hill, but it had interesting things in it that she had gathered over the years. Not at all gloomy as she sometimes appeared, Jessie was a lively storyteller, often telling jokes on herself. That night over fried chicken she told me of a period in her life during which she had undergone an emotional crisis. She was living with a relative, a cousin, I believe, in New York City. And one day her relative came in and started scolding her: "You sit around here all the time and you never go anywhere. Why don't you get out and go?"

Jessie said that it hurt her feelings so much that the next day she went to a travel agency there in New York, walked in, and asked the man, "What's the farthest place I can go from New York City, right now?"

He named a spot on the Indian Ocean, and Jessie said,

"That's where I want to go. Give me a ticket." And she went.

Jessie remarked that the chicken didn't have any salt on it, but that I could add some if I liked. She had high blood pressure, she said, and was having trouble getting it down and keeping it down. The chicken tasted all right to me, and I didn't really take seriously her remark about high blood pressure, for it is very commonplace among blacks in the South, and I was surprised that she was so concerned about it. Now, of course, health personnel have done a good job of alerting the black population to the dangers of untreated hypertension.

In the coming weeks I saw Jessie often. Though I was frequently depressed and felt that the future held little for me, talking with her always helped. Once she asked me to go with her to see a play the campus theater was presenting and another time she came over to Durham to have supper with me. I was now sharing an apartment with two NCC faculty women near the college.

We must have seemed an odd couple, a tall, rawboned, sandy-haired white North Carolinian and a tall, stocky, dark North Carolinian, but then maybe not, for this was the high tide of the civil rights movement in the South. But then Jessie was the type who wouldn't have cared if someone had stared.

Jessie was very high-spirited one evening and told me stories of her years in New York, the years between twenty and thirty-five, which she said were the best years to spend in the City. She spoke of friends whom she knew then. I told her that I was very lonely and wanted to marry, but it seemed that I never would. She said that she didn't see why not, for I was very beautiful. I was startled at that, for few people saw beauty when they looked at me. She said that she could "marry tomorrow" if she wanted to, but that she didn't want to.

As the weeks passed and we talked, I continued to get a look into the world Jessie inhabited, which to me was that of the Woman Writer. One day she told me about a weekend that she and several friends had spent at the beach. It was off-season and, from the way she described it, very lonely, with its own special kind of beauty in the winter. I never knew until then that people went to the beach in the winter. I don't know what I thought happened to the beach when it was cold.

Jessie was a real professional and talked candidly of writing and writers. Some of her comments on contemporary writers whom she had known gave me a different view of them. I had been so oriented to "literature" that I forgot that there were very real men and women writing it. In talking to Jessie, however, I realized that a writer has the freedom to use things from his own experience in his writing and often does. That was a revelation to me. I don't know where I thought that plots and characters in novels came from, but I didn't think that they came from the writer's own life. After this, writing seemed even more like magic, and very powerful. For if you were a writer there was nothing in your experience that you could not at some time put into your writing. At that time in Chapel Hill some referred to writing as a craft; others referred to it as an art. I still like to think of it as powerful magic. If a writer can evoke the right sequence of sounds, meanings, tone, rhythm, and that indefinable something that turns words into feeling and thoughts, then he or she has become the most powerful sorcerer of them all.

Faust wished for the wrong things. He should have sold his soul for the ability to write extremely well.

One day while we were having lunch Jessie told me of a cousin who had recently died in an area hospital after a minor operation. The surgeon who had operated on her had failed to tie some sutures properly, and she had been left alone for a long time and had bled to death. Jessie had gone to the hospital several times, trying to get something done about it, but the doctors had closed ranks behind the man she held responsible for her cousin's death, and there was nothing she could do about it. She was very upset and talked during the meal of the indifference of modern medicine and how it allowed a woman to bleed to death, when just a few visits during the postoperative period might have saved her life. She told me that she was writing a book about it, called "The Surgeon."

I didn't see Jessie for a while after that. Once she sent me a card from Pennsylvania, where she was visiting friends, saying that she had had to go away for a while, for her blood pressure had gotten high again. I paid a little more attention to the matter, but still the full impact of it didn't strike me. When next I saw her, she told me that she felt better, but that she was going out to San Francisco to see a friend of hers, a woman who was also a writer. She sent me another card from California, and I was pleased that she had written, for I knew then that she considered me a friend.

The days passed and I tried to work around my emotional pain, doing some work on good days, missing several days when I felt bad, but mainly wondering which way to go. Once I got a doctorate, where was I going with it? Back to a place like North Carolina College? I didn't want that, yet I didn't seem to have the will, the drive to plan a life, to set a goal I wanted to reach. At that time I was just hoping to hang on, and my goal was to try not to go completely over the edge if I could help it.

The integrationist fervor of the sixties turned to concern about Vietnam on the one hand and to black consciousness and black power on the other; Jessie had evidenced an interest in both. In one of our last conversations she told me that she had applied to go to Vietnam for a year—to teach in Saigon. She had made definite plans, knew which hotel she would be staying at, and had made some contacts with other Americans who were in Saigon. For a moment I felt a longing again to get away. I had once made plans to spend many years out of the United States, but I had never followed through on any of them.

One day Jessie discussed with me the work of a young African writer from Tanganyika. She was so impressed with one of his stories that she had included it in a short story collection that she edited. The story concerned a young man who was trying to make a decision between the West and the East, as to which type of government he felt that his country should follow, now that it had its independence. He becomes disillusioned with America and at the end catches a plane to Peking. Jessie sounded so enthusiastic about the story and the young man's talent that I got a copy of the book just to read it. I read the story with a strange feeling—a growing belief that I could write one just as good. But I was fearful, and still did not try.

One night, while the television was on, I heard that Jessie had died at her home. I immediately thought of the high blood pressure and wondered if that was the cause of her death, but I never found out.

I have since regretted that when Jessie reached out to me, I was not yet free enough to accept her friendship completely. I had yet to learn in my life that the hardest thing for me to do is not to reach out to find a friend, but to be able to accept and respond when friendship is extended. Not until the seventies would I gain enough confidence in myself to be able to respond positively when someone evidently thought I was a real all-right person.

I wonder sometimes what effect meeting Jessie had on my later development. I suspect that in using her as a model, subconsciously I saw greater possibilities for myself. The things she told me about the private lives of the writers she knew convinced me, very deep inside, in the place just before thoughts form, that perhaps by writing about it, I might make my world more intelligible too.

To my knowledge "The Surgeon" was never published.

15

August 1967: I was going into the Deep South, to Orangeburg, South Carolina, to accept a position at South Carolina State College, at that time still mainly for black students only. This bus ride to me was a climactic experience. It meant change. Something had happened in my life, and after five years at North Carolina College I was leaving. More accurate was the fact that *nothing* was happening in my life, and I was leaving, trying to make something happen. Life had to have some meaning. It was written.

All my passivity, all my endurance had not given my life any meaning, had not made something happen—that mysterious "something" that would make all the pain worth the price. What was it, that mysterious something? I would give anything to find it, but having searched in every place I could think of, I had become convinced that "it" didn't exist. But there was always that still small voice, that feeling inside me that said, Try one more time. That voice had been the bane of my life. Just when I had almost reached the peace of total resignation to life as it was and was determined not to try anymore, the voice said, Try one more time. Maybe if you pursue this course, you will win. Maybe. Try. It whispered ever so softly, yet it was insistent. Try. Try. Try.

My reading problem was not as bad as it had been, and when I could I would study another subject; read on my own in some field where I was a blank; or go out to hear what the newest ideas "going down" were about. Try. Try. Try. There's got to be a way out. There's got to be. Try. The other voice said, Give up; this is all there is. Get a new car and forget it. But the first voice said, Try. Try. Try. And the war within me nearly tore me apart.

I found an apartment adjacent to the campus. Actually, it was a room in an old house with shared kitchen and living room. My roommates were a public-school teacher and a colleague at South Carolina State.

Orangeburg had a town square. There was a small park in the middle of it, ringed with parking meters, the insignia of the twentieth century. Forming an inner ring to the parking meters were several glossy magnolia trees, the insignia of the Deep South. Squarely in the middle of the park, the statue of the man in gray, that lonely sentinel of a thousand Southern towns that could not believe that they had lost the Civil War, looked south, down Main Street. It was on such a tall superstructure of concrete "erected by the women of Orangeburg County" that the soldier stood just under the fluttering Confederate flag that shared the municipal flagpole with the Stars and Stripes—some hundred years after Lee had surrendered. On the statue was an inscription:

A GRATEFUL TRIBUTE
TO THE BRAVE DEFENDERS OF
OUR RIGHTS
OUR HONOR AND
OUR HOMES

The soldier was guarded by two cannons, one on either side, pointing toward Main Street. These cannons must have been powerless on the day that the Union troops came through—as the marker by the Confederate soldier attests: "Courthouse Sq. Destroyed by Union Troops during their Occupation Feb. 12–13, 1865."

The Confederate soldier and the cannon guarding him looked past the towers of the two radio stations in the town, both of which were hostile to the black population of the county. To get information about the weather, time, and the price of crops, the blacks had to listen to these stations or not listen at all. There were no black-oriented stations in the area.

So the Confederate soldier, his cannons, and his flag guarded both radio stations—and also the newspaper, which was just a block away.

He dominated other aspects of Orangeburg life as well. On his right was Commerce, represented by J. C. Penney and the bank. On his left, Religion, represented by a huge brick building with Greek columns which dominated one side of the square, the First Baptist Church. Behind him, his reign continued: S. H. Kress and, hard by, the white-bricked, medieval-looking, turreted Methodist Church. Though Orangeburg County was fifty percent black, the soldier from one hundred years ago still ruled the territory, and his statue spoke of guarding "Our Rights." No black citizen of the town had the slightest doubt of whose rights he was meant to defend—they certainly weren't theirs. The flag that was still flying over blacks' heads in 1967 had once waved over the heads of thousands of men who went to war to insure that blacks would always be slaves.

Though he was meant to protect "Our Rights, Our Honor, and Our Homes" from the blacks, the Confederate soldier didn't mind helping the blacks spend their money. On Saturday, Commerce thrived. The town square teemed with blacks. They crowded Kress's, fingering the glittering jewelry, glamorous cosmetics, and plastic handbags. Some of the more sophisticated sat at the lunch counters and ordered Cokes, a privilege that had been denied them by Orangeburg merchants a few years earlier. Orangeburg always had the American money ethic. Money was good—take anybody's money. So the blacks in those earlier days had been welcomed for their nickels and dimes and crumpled dollars. But they were denied the amusements or pleasures that meant they were people with feelings—simple pleasures, like sitting at a lunch counter. This denial persisted until the blacks denied the merchants their dollars by not entering their stores. Boycott.

Girls with Afro hairdos and a little bit more money strolled into J. C. Penney's and looked at what Washington, D.C., and New York City thought fashionable—last year or the year before. It took at least a year for new fashions to drift South.

Some blacks had money in their pockets, some just looked, but all were welcomed with politeness and sometimes with a smile. The next day the square teemed with whites: not a black face was to be seen. For it was Sunday, the Lord's day, and blacks were not welcome to attend the churches in the square.

Two blocks from the square, between Kress's and the South Carolina State campus, was a bowling alley, the principal source of amusement in town other than the two movie houses. The bowling alley was "private," or so the owner said. What he really meant was "For Whites Only." It was located in a shopping center where blacks went to buy groceries and shoes and hardware. But bowl? Never. So the college students who went to the A&P for Ritz crackers and sardines and huge

184

bottles of Coke were forced to walk right on by the all-white bowling alley.

The college semester began. I met my new classes, mainly freshmen, mainly from the low country, with a few New Yorkers thrown in for good measure.

In black Southern colleges there are always a scattering of Northerners. Most of them are children of Southerners who have gone North, but retained a tie with parents, relatives, and friends in the South. So when the child finishes high school in the North, the parents send him or her South to college. Sometimes they send their children down to stay with their grandparents; and they register as citizens of the state, thus avoiding out-of-state tuition. I thought for a long time that this financial benefit was the overwhelming reason why Northern children chose to come South to black colleges. But then I learned that tuition in some municipal colleges in the New York area was very low or even nonexistent. So there had to be another reason. I thought that it might be academic competition—that the Northerners thought that they might not be able to hold their own with whites in the city. Although I thought and still think that was part of the answer, it was not all. In the final analysis it seemed to be a combination of things: it was less expensive to go South to a black college, it was easier academically, and it was fun. There was a feeling of camaraderie among the Southern blacks that many Northern blacks seemed to like.

I had taught freshman English for several years now, but I still did not know what to do. For my students were not writers. I had often heard black students referred to as nonverbal, but that was not the case. They talked a great deal. It was the transfer of speech to paper that stymied them. To facilitate the transfer was the task I set for myself.

I taught English and tuned in to the ambiance of the place, looked at television, and in general kept pretty much to myself.

For I was weary of trying to find a place where I fit in, with people to whom I could talk, with whom I could share ideas.

My isolation from people was still close to total. But my interest in the world around me remained keen and alive. I wanted
to know. Who? What? When? Where? Why? What was going
on in the world? What was going on on the campus? What
was stirring in the community? I kept hearing about a conflict
between the town and the students, over the bowling alley.

I came in to Orangeburg on the wave of black consciousness
that had been unleashed by the Voting Rights March through
Mississippi in the summer of 1965—the summer that saw
black fists shoot into the air and the strains of "Black Power"
echo on that hot dusty march. Feelings were unleashed that
had been pent up for many generations. Black consciousness
came to the fore in American life. Things identified with the
black peasants became the "in" things, the accepted things.
Other facets of black life were ignored at best or denounced at
worst. Things associated with the black folk were called
"soul," a term that meant the indefinable essence of a people.

Food had to be soul food. This was the food eaten by the
blacks when they didn't have the money to buy anything better. This food was heavy in animal fat, particularly pork fat.
Neckbones, pigs' tails, pigs' feet, pigs' ears, pigs' intestines
(chitterlings), and spareribs became *de rigueur*. Because the
blacks had eaten the leavings of the hog after the white plan-
tation owner had taken the best for his family, such food had
become associated with the life of the black folk. The irony of
the situation was that by the 1960s, many of the black folk
had become affluent enough to try another diet, and those
who didn't often suffered the consequences of a diet heavy in
animal fat—high blood pressure. So while health personnel
everywhere were trying to turn the black folk from the food
that had wreaked havoc on the health of the population,
young college-trained blacks were busy trying to reintroduce
such items in their diet to prove they had "soul." College di-
eticians were approached and back came the pork items in the
college cafeterias, along with some other specialties of the region: turnip greens and collard greens, black-eyed peas, and
pinto beans. Even at some white universities with substantial

black enrollments, the dining halls introduced soul food weeks, so that the whole university community had the privilege of dining on soul food. Duke University in Durham was one such institution.

Along with the return to soul food came the glorification of the African features of American blacks. Natural super-curly hair was highlighted among both young men and young women, with the growing popularity of the Afro hairdo. The change was most startling among the girls. While black girls used to have their hair straightened with a hot comb at a very early age, often as young as five or six, a process that continued through a lifetime, young black women in the mid-sixties in the United States started wearing their hair in its natural unstraightened state.

When the Afro was first introduced among black women, it was not so attractive, but as time went by women learned various ways of treating unstraightened hair, and with the introduction of the "Afro comb" or "pick," the grooming of such styles improved. The pick was really a multipronged wide fork that lifted the hair from the head in such a way that it could be styled. Often the wearer of the Afro plaited her hair in braids at night and combed it out in the morning. In the seventies, some young women started wearing the plaits all day. Where there had been only one style—straightened hair—there were now three—straightened hair, unstraightened Afro, and braided hair, often "corn-rowed" into intricate patterns.

The young men followed suit, though the change for them was not as extreme. Straightened hair had never been as widespread among men as among women. It had been confined mainly to the lowest strata of the black community in the larger Northern urban centers. Most black males wore their hair in its natural state, but short. With the advent of the mid-sixties, however, they started wearing their hair longer and then longer and even longer, until it often rivaled the girls' in length. (Later, in the early seventies, when the girls started corn-rowing their hair, some of the young men followed suit.)

The academic year moved on—football, pep rallies, classes.

And the gold and blue days that were fall in Orangeburg deepened into a rather mild winter, really more like fall with a gray filter over it.

My classes met, and I talked with the students and read papers and went home and watched TV and wondered about my life and how it turned out so full of disappointment. For was not life meant to be more? Then I reminded myself that I had a job while many people did not, and that I could buy things that I needed and some that I wanted. But that didn't comfort me for long. I wanted more out of life.

Christmas came and went, and the students' murmuring about the bowling alley grew louder. They sent their secret weapon, a white male student, to test the "members only" policy of the lanes and found that he could go in whenever he wanted to, but the black students couldn't. They were angered, and soon students began going to the alley to protest.

One night on TV I saw and heard an interview with the owner of the bowling alley. I heard the subliminal message in his statements. The owner was a slight, passive-looking man whose way of dressing and speaking said a great deal. What I read into his comments was: "All my life the only advantage that I've ever had is that I am white. My mother and father didn't have anything, but I've managed to obtain a little something in this world. That helps me cement my position as being one with the other whites of Orangeburg, some of whom have money, others of whom have family name, and others of whom, starting out with no more than I have, now have college educations. My family didn't have money. My father worked hard all his life; my mother did too. I didn't have a prestigious family name. We were one of the mass of white working poor. I wasn't fortunate enough to get a college education.

"But there's one thing I do have—a white skin—and thus I am joined with other whites. Therefore, I am a member of the community. I have a place. I belong. I must never do anything to lose that place, that one advantage, because without it I am lost. If blacks go to the five-and-ten-cent store and want to eat, the manager says nothing. Why should he? He doesn't stand to lose anything. Kress's or Woolworth's all have many branches in far distant cities. So the manager does not lose face if a black customer appears and wants to eat. He is a part of the twentieth-century mass of young executives who move from city to city, following their companies. He has his own social set, his own standards, his own milieu. Thus, the surrounding community cannot pressure him. It is not his store; his home office is in New York or Atlanta.

"But I, who have nothing, cannot afford to do that. If I let them in my bowling alley, I will lose face. I cannot move away and I will have nothing to prove that I am a bona fide member of the white race. Therefore, let them come as much as they want to, I'll not let them in to bowl. As long as I have the power to deny, be it ever so small, that proves that I, as a white man, am in a better position than the blacks. Once I lose the power to deny, I have lost everything."

So four years after the Civil Rights Public Accommodation Act of 1964, which supposedly gave blacks the privilege of spending their money where they chose to in public facilities, one lone figure was holding out, and he planned to hold out forever. He was to become an obsession of the black student community at Orangeburg. The black folk didn't much care—bowling wasn't their "thing." The students didn't particularly care for bowling, either. It wasn't part of their parents' life-style; it wasn't a part of their own life-style. But protest against racial discrimination was an integral part of their life-style. The owner misjudged the situation.

There were student demonstrations night after night. They gave me an eerie feeling. This was the late sixties, but the protest had the flavor of the early sixties in Durham and other towns across the South.

One night during a demonstration in front of the alley, a window was broken in the crush. The manager called the police. The police and the firemen responded—the police with

189

swinging billy clubs, the firemen with water hoses. The crowd fell back, enraged, and on its way back to the campus some left evidence of their rage, mainly smashed windows. The town called on the Governor to help them, and the Governor backed the town by sending in the National Guard.

Heavily armed Ku Klux Klansmen drove in from the surrounding county and parked in the lot in front of the bowling alley, as if to dare any black to appear there. The police took no notice of them.

The John Birch Society took a full-page ad in the local newspaper to warn that the demonstration was a Communist plot. It seems that the men in the Kremlin had heard of Orangeburg, South Carolina, and plotted to destroy it, for some reason that will forever remain obscure. The press itself was not a model of accurate, unbiased reporting.

So the town simmered.

In town at the Holiday Inn were National Guardsmen and the Highway Patrol. They ate and slept and watched television.

Tension crackled everywhere. The big eruption came on February 8, 1968, the night of the Orangeburg incident.

I was asleep during most of it, but around ten o'clock that night, I awakened to the sound of many car doors closing. The sound was muffled, as though they were being closed far away. I thought that perhaps there was a party in the tavern across the yard, which was set back from the street. Something was wrong, though, for I didn't hear the noisy shouts that usually accompanied activity at the tavern. I drifted back off to sleep, but not for long, for the sound was so regular that I knew that a lot of cars were gathering somewhere. I got up to see what the matter was. I looked out of the curtained door and was amazed. The whole street was lined with cars. That was the muffled sound that I had heard—the people in the cars were closing the doors softly.

Not turning on the light, I went and stood on the porch. I could see activity in a little shop nearby. It had been a barber-

190

shop; now it was used by the community. I put on my house-coat and my bedroom shoes and went across the lawn to the shop.

When I opened the door I stood for a moment, not knowing what to say, for the room was full of men and it was very quiet. "What's the matter?" I said. No one said anything. I was beginning to be able to see a little better in the dim light. That's when I noticed a man talking on the telephone. He was not really talking, but rather holding the telephone as though he was waiting for someone to come back to answer. "What's the matter?" I said again. No one said anything. For one wild moment I thought of saying, "If you don't tell me, I am going to call the police." The shop was in our yard and was used for the voter-education project. I slept in the front of the house, and many times I had been afraid, for if hostile whites decided to "hit" the shop, the blast would have shattered the glass in my room; or they perhaps could miscalculate and hit the house.

Finally one man spoke. "We're trying to call the Governor," he said. "They're up there on campus, killing our students."

I heard him, but I didn't hear him. He had just given me a piece of information that I couldn't process. "Killing our students?" I said.

"Yes, that old Highway Patrol opened fire on them tonight."

I stood there for a moment, unbelieving, and then started across the lawn. Halfway to my house I got sick, and I stayed sick all night.

They couldn't find the Governor, yet twenty-one hours later, he was on statewide television giving an "official" version of the incident. That was a mistake, and he had to spend the rest of his term justifying this "official" version.

When I talked to my students about it later, they told me that between ten and ten-thirty p.m., many of them had gone down to the front of the campus to see a bonfire that some students had started. A fire truck arrived, and police and state

191

troopers came up on the grass, so the students started to turn back toward the boys' dormitory. Then someone said, "Don't move, because we haven't done anything, and they aren't coming up on our campus."

But the patrolmen did start coming toward them on campus, some from the street and others from the yard of the house on tbe corner adjacent to the campus. At this most of the students began backing up. Then a policeman fell to the ground. A whistle blew, then a shot was fired. It was said that none of the students had fired.

The first shot triggered an outburst of firing, and the students ran toward the dormitory. Some fell on the ground when the shooting started, and at first they thought that the patrolmen were shooting over their heads. But when they heard the groans of their classmates who had been struck by bullets, they knew that the opposite was true.

A second whistle blew, and the shooting stopped. One student fell and couldn't move. Five or six patrolmen came up and prodded him with their sticks, as if to see if he could move. When he didn't, they grabbed him by his hands and feet and dragged him to the edge of the campus and down the grassy knoll. They beat him, hitting him over and over. Some students had run to the unoccupied house and remained there until after the shooting. The police dragged them out of the house and beat them also.

Later, when faculty and townspeople and students arrived at Orangeburg Regional Hospital with the wounded—and three dead—the troopers told them to lay the wounded students on the "damn" floor. The nurses showed their hostility to the students by making sarcastic remarks.

America did not respond. There was no nationwide student strike. Three black students had died trying to use a bowling alley one block from their campus.

The Governor closed the school for an indefinite period (it lasted several weeks) and ringed the black community with

192

troops. They established checkpoints and behaved in other ways like an occupation army. I went back to Durham during the interim, sick at heart. I had a long time to think about Orangeburg and what had happened there.

One thing became clear: the rhetoric had changed, but the tactics hadn't. The integrationist rhetoric of the early sixties—"We shall overcome" and "Black and white together"—had given way to the black power rhetoric of the middle and late sixties, but this new black power movement had not yet developed strategies to go along with the new political stance. So when the situation about the bowling alley developed, they fell back on the old tactics of demonstrations. Passive resistance had had an entirely different philosophy and contingency plans. The black power philosophy had not yet worked out any plans. Although the civil rights movement had been fueled by college students, it had quickly ignited the bulk of the black population, and then it couldn't die, for the black folk wouldn't let it. The black power proponents, however, had not yet hit on a medium or a message that would appeal to and awaken a large number of the black folk, and so it stayed largely on the campus. Two major problems, then, of black power had not yet been solved. (1) What strategy should be used in actual situations in dealing with instances of white injustice? (2) How do you involve masses of black folk?

There was more to the Orangeburg incident than met the eye. It concerns the role played by the "adults" at the College.

First, the presidency was up for grabs. The former president had made a tumultuous exit after a student revolt the previous year. There was now an acting president. Many wanted the job and there was a lot of jockeying for it.

The former president himself was an interesting case. Physically indistinguishable from a white man, he was a patrician in manner and attitude. A graduate of Harvard, he once told a black faculty member that it distressed him that Harvard had started admitting so many blacks; he felt it would cheapen the

193

degree. This man did not mingle socially with other people at the College—neither the Light Skins nor the Dark Skins. The Light Skins didn't mind that he seemed distant to the Dark Skins, but were enraged that he was distant to *them*. Thus, his departure from the campus was not mourned. I saw him once in the summer of 1965, when I taught one summer session at the College. He spoke to me—first—on the porch of the campus post office. I was so amazed when he spoke—I had heard many negative stories—that it took me a while to think to say "good evening" back to him.

Next and, I feel, more devastating was the matter of the "country club." Some people at the College organized it and it was alleged that the membership was chosen arbitrarily: this one, not that one. You and you, step forward; you and you, go back. Neither rank nor length of service to the College nor any other discernible standard of selection was used. It tore the social fabric of the campus apart. It was the subject of never-ending talk: who was invited and who wasn't. The talk went on in the dining room, in the post office, on the sidewalks, everywhere. Thus, while the students were challenging the "membership only" policy of the bowling alley, the "adults" were preoccupied by a "country club."

I think that anyone who wants to understand the history of blacks in America should take a careful look at the Orangeburg incident. Basically, three groups were involved. There were those working for change in the status of blacks: the young people, the students. There were the intransigent white racists, determined that there would be no change, not if they could help it. And there were the black "leaders," sowing seeds of dissension, mistrust, and hatred among their own kind by trying to establish a class within a class.

The sixties reeled and stumbled and fell to a close. Many things changed, many didn't. But one thing was sure: There was no one in America, no institution, that was unaffected by that era.

In the spring of 1968, in addition to a Southern Fellowships Fund grant, I had a teaching assistantship at the University of North Carolina. Once again I returned to the Chapel Hill campus.

16

It was a beautiful autumn day in Chapel Hill, just before Thanksgiving, 1968. The sky was a special postcard blue, and clouds drifted over the red-brick dormitories like cookie-shaped puffs of smoke. There were few leaves on the ground. Evidently when each leaf fell a yardman quickly and invisibly whisked it away. The trees—dogwoods, I thought—had hundreds of skinny arms, and they all looked to be the same height. Here and there a dry, mud-colored leaf stuck as though it were glued on. I liked the walk from the dormitory to the library.

So I walked along, through the unpaved parking lot with mud holes in the reddish sand in front of the modern building—the student union—all glass and concrete and squat, just as if a whole basketball team had stood on all sides and mashed it down. It had two sister buildings next to it, a bookstore and a library. I walked past them, but a feeling that had been nibbling at the corners of my spirit came through to my conscious mind: I want to get away. But I walked along and forced myself toward the building that I loved—the library, with its huge dome. I used to go into the reference room and look up at the chandelier suspended high from the ceiling. It made me feel in awe; I had a tendency to whisper there. I noticed that other people had a tendency to whisper too. Across the hall in the magazine room the ceiling was lower, and I was more relaxed there; people spoke louder there too. I loved every bit of the library and knew most of it. I always liked entering the stacks—it was semi-dark there and quiet, and I felt at home. I spent many hours reading the titles of books on the shelves. I read row after row of titles. Sometimes I felt that I had read the spine of nearly every book in the library.

So I walked toward the cherished library, but I still wanted to leave. Even as I walked up the stone steps, looking down carefully as I always did since one icy day when I had slipped and fallen, I noticed the depressions in each step showing where many footsteps had trod, while around the huge columns supporting the portico the stone was unworn and dark from disuse.

I walked, looking down, then went through the narrow swinging doors, too narrow for such a big building, such heavy traffic. Why did I want to leave? I felt dead all over.

I walked past the tall columns in the lobby and up the stairs leading to the second floor and headed through the entrance to the stacks. Then I waited for the elevator down to my carrel, where I clicked on the light in the quiet, cool darkness, sat on my pillow, put my head down, and started to cry.

I decided to visit "Miss Louella" in Pittsburgh. She was the widow of one of my mother's old cousins. I saw in my mind's eye her full, smooth, black laughing face, with crooked teeth, tiny black moles on either side of her nose, so small they looked like little black freckles, and a jet-black pageboy wig that fell to her shoulders. Her ankles were swollen, so she wore "old slides" all the time and her legs had bulging veins from holding up her heavy form for so many years. She laughed a lot, swore a lot, and told outrageous jokes.

I thought it would be a relief to get away from the University for a while—even the cool and quiet of the library and the smell of books that I loved—and hear some laughter and jokes at her house. Miss Louella wouldn't care about books, and I doubted if she could even read. I thought about her bawdy jests and jibes, and I laughed to myself.

They knew I was coming, but at ten-thirty p.m. the house looked dark, withdrawn, foreboding. I had tried to call at the bus station, but the line was busy. The whole block looked dark, dingy, isolated, and deserted, as though the tenants had been told to move for urban renewal. A few lights flickered in oddly spaced windows. But the sidewalks were dirty and I saw no one.

I asked the taxi driver to wait while I checked to see if there was anybody home. He was a good-looking light-brown man, Afro-haired, unthreatening, about twenty-five or twenty-six. At first no one answered my knock. But then my cousin Cat's full-moon face appeared, accompanied by the blast of the record player in the front room and laughter and noise in the inner room. I went back to the cab, got my things, and tipped the driver a dollar.

There was Miss Louella in a wig that flowed down her back, black face with black freckles, smiling at me. She was presiding over a table that had two awfully small bottles of Scotch on it, around which sat men and women laughing and talking. I was introduced as her "cousin's daughter who teaches school." At last I was home, away from the sterility of the library stacks at Chapel Hill, back to the roots, the warmth, the laughter of blackness. I was going to laugh and enjoy myself, and maybe on Monday when I went back to UNC I would be renewed and refreshed, recapturing the vitality of spirit that had completely seeped out of me.

So I sat there and smiled and wondered why Miss Louella didn't offer me some food. I had ridden nearly eight hours on the bus; it was close to eleven, and I hadn't had anything to eat since noon. Still she sat, and I wondered. At home in the South, it was understood that a visitor was to be fed, and when company was coming from a long way, a dinner was prepared.

So I was embarrassed at having to say, "Miss Louella, I'm hungry," right there in front of everybody. Men, women, a baby, her relatives, their friends. But I did. As I followed her out into the kitchen, I was glad to put a wall between me and the noise. The kitchen was dominated by a huge refrigerator—Miss Louella was always the cook in the family. Miss Louella had dozens of fish, and she explained that she was going to have a selling tomorrow for some friends. I wondered at this, but thought it would be delightful to participate in a Saturday night fish fry. The fish I ate now was too salty. I had eaten institutional food too long, and that's why the taste was too much. After I had had some sleep, there would be laughter and good times tomorrow.

I knew something was wrong when the next morning Miss Louella called me and silently pressed some bills in my hand.

"This is the money for the chickens," she said. "George is coming around this afternoon and he'll take you to buy them."

I looked at her, wondering what in the world was the matter.

"They're for the selling tonight," she said.

I still couldn't make heads or tails of what was going on. I wondered about Cat and Clyde, her grown-up children, living at home and working every day. Why didn't they help Miss Louella with her selling? Cat had had many husbands, and now, a grandmother before she was forty, she was keeping her daughter's child; her daughter was busy dancing in a rock-and-roll singer's revue, so Cat said. Clyde had never been married and had never left home. He worked on a furniture truck.

Miss Louella saw me staring at her and whispered, "Clyde only gives me ten dollars a week, and that doesn't even buy enough food to feed him, let alone anybody else in the house, and Cat gets to drinking in the bar and that's where her money goes, all that she doesn't give to her friends."

"Friends?" I said.

"Her men friends," she said. "We had a hundred-dollar telephone bill last month and I don't know how we're going to pay it, and the rent's due and I haven't got the money. That's why I'm having this little selling, trying to make the rent. I'm afraid to give the money to Cat. She'll get rid of it for me and I won't have my chickens."

I thought, Rent party! Rent parties were something that used to happen in black urban communities during the Depression. I didn't know they still had them. But then we heard Cat stirring, so I took the money and said nothing.

"Come on, Cuz," Cat said. "Let's go to the bar."

Bar, I thought. People have hardly gotten out of bed and you're going to a bar. But I said nothing and went along—after all, I was the guest.

We got to the bar while the owner was still sweeping and washing off the counter. He greeted us heartily, and it was easy to tell that Cat was an old and faithful customer.

Clyde and Slim came in, and Cat and Clyde acted as if Slim were their brother. I had noticed him at Miss Louella's the night before, when he seemed to be one of the family, going into the kitchen frequently and laughing and joking with Miss Louella. He wore a sailor's hat to cover a deeply receding hairline.

They ordered drinks, and the bartender put down his broom and fixed them. I had orange juice. Slim and Clyde went over to the jukebox and selected some records. Soon a bunch of people came in, evidently all regulars, for they called each other by nicknames and reminisced at great length and tremendous volume about things that had taken place on other occasions when they were together. I listened to the music and sipped my orange juice and tried to feel that I was one of the group. After all, these were my cousins and the others were their friends, and this is how they relaxed on the weekend. There was nothing wrong with going to the bar in the morning, I really felt. But then I remembered that Miss Louella had given me the money to buy the chickens because she didn't trust her own daughter with it, and Miss Louella needed to have a selling to raise money to pay her rent, though Clyde was right there drinking and playing the jukebox and horsing around. Something was wrong in this situation. But I tried to quiet my doubts, for I, too, had been caught up in the "return to the roots" movement of the mid-sixties. I overlooked the fact that my roots were the agrarian South, not urbanized centers like Pittsburgh, and that this milieu was alien to me.

I don't know when she left, but I looked up and Cat was

199

gone—just vanished out of the bar. I remembered that the last time I looked over, she'd been talking to a tall, stocky young man, holding her drink and laughing up in his face. I wondered if he was one of the men Miss Louella meant when she said that Cat had men that she gave money to. I sat and waited and waited, but Cat didn't come back. Though I was sure we couldn't have been too far from Miss Louella's, I didn't know the way back. Clyde said that he was going out for a minute with one of his friends, and he left with a group of leather-jacketed young men, all of them with the processed hair known as a "conk." I was rather startled by that. Black college students were very much into the "black folk" tradition, yet they wore neither leather jackets nor "conks"; they wore Afros and denim. I had observed before that sometimes what college students designate as "folk" and what the sure-enough "folk" actually practice sometimes differ by light years.

The man called Slim came over and sat and talked, about how good Miss Louella had been to him, and how he felt a part of the family. He was separated from his wife and child. He worked as a janitor in a school nearby, and he showed me the stub of his paycheck, which was for seventy-five dollars. I realized that he was quite proud of his pay, and I said that that was a whole lot of money. That seemed to please him a good deal.

After a while Slim said, "Let's go somewhere where we can talk; it's too noisy here."

I had to agree, for by now the bar had filled with people dressed up as though it were nighttime. Everybody seemed to know everybody else, and the noise was deafening. The bartender, knowing what his patrons wanted, had the jukebox turned up loud, and the only pause in the music occurred during the brief intervals when the machine changed records.

Slim suggested that we go to his apartment, for he suspected that Cat was not going to return that morning. I suspected so too. I hesitated, but he acted offended. Why shouldn't I go?

We could talk there. Miss Louella was the best friend that he had in this world; she had helped him out he didn't know how many times. Something told me not to go, but the same something that had sent me away from the University, seeking the warmth and laughter of the black folk, said, "There you go again, scorning the life-style of the folk. That's what's wrong with you; you've gotten too far away from your roots." People actually talked like that in black communities at that time.

I walked with him through the Pittsburgh streets on a gray damp Saturday morning. He carried on a conversation about his tour in the Air Force, the places he'd seen overseas, his hometown of Atlanta.

When we got to his place, I heard music. Then I realized that he let the radio play all day, for he didn't want to come home to an environment devoid of sound. Before I got in the door, something told me that it was a mistake. Like an animal I sensed danger, and I turned to go. I was too late. He attacked me.

The most horrifying thing about a rape scene is that it is unesthetic. It is without grace. I didn't think of an unwanted pregnancy; I thought of some filthy disease being implanted deep inside me that I would never be rid of—some filth, some slime that would last forever.

I remember feeling deep cold when the voice changed and I saw my blouse tear. From the corner of my eye I saw the kitchen table and thought of the knife that was probably somewhere near, but the cool mind that I have cautioned me that to introduce a knife into a situation like that would mean serious injury or death to me.

I ceased thinking of Slim as a human being; to me he became and remains a nothing. As a nothing, I had no feelings toward him. He could get shot down, run over, whatever, and I would not care. He could live a long and happy life and I would not care. To me he simply is not a part of the human family.

When I told Miss Louella about it, I was disappointed in her

201

reaction. She did not act surprised and only said, "Don't let Cat know." While I was still trying to absorb this information she let slip a remark about Slim that led me to believe that she too knew more about him than she should have. No wonder Slim loved the family.

I bought the fresh chickens and later paid for my supper. Then I said good-bye forever to Pittsburgh, and the way of life it represented.

I no longer felt the nagging sense of guilt that I used to feel when someone said, "You still going to school. When you going to finish? That's all you do, go to school." I no longer felt guilt when someone said, "All you know is what's in books; when are you going to learn something about life?" The guilt that I did feel, however, was that I was happier at the University than I had yet been anywhere. Nobody called me in and warned me of the danger of wearing stripes with plaids; I could write a paper that disagreed with the professor's opinion and not get a failing grade because my point of view differed. I was glad to escape the constant criticism at home, the indifference of North Carolina College at Durham, the sterility of the high school where I had taught. Guilt fled. No more guilt because I made my living reading and writing rather than putting tobacco on the belt. I was what I was. I accepted it; other people would have to. The black folk had had something when they lived the simple, agrarian life in the South. Depending largely on the land for a living, they were church-centered and family-oriented; there was a degree of cohesion in the community. But upon their remove to the cities something had happened to lessen those bonds, and the results were not nice to see. So on my way back to the "folk" I had been stopped in mid-flight by the reality of the situation. That was another avenue cut off from me. What I would do, the only thing I could do, was live a marginal existence, until some change permitted another kind of existence. What that something was I didn't know. But I would hang on and see.

The attorney whom I consulted after I got back to Chapel

Hill, once he found that I was absolutely not going to press charges against Slim, advised me to write a detailed account of the incident and send it to the district attorney in Pittsburgh, for he had responsibilities to all the people. Then, too, the case could be opened at some later date. I wrote the letter. I guess the district attorney still has it in his files.

Part

FIVE

17

I probably will never know why one day, after looking at the current issue of the *North Carolina Anvil*, a weekly published in the Durham–Chapel Hill–Raleigh area, I decided to write for it. I think that it may have had something to do with the fact that its orientation was different from that of other newspapers around: "Politics and the Arts" was part of its motto. It also published short stories. But regardless of the reason, I set down a piece, handwritten on large file cards. Then I got into my battered Chevy II and drove over from Chapel Hill to Durham. The *Anvil* offices were located in the back of a printing shop. Bob Brown, the editor, came out to see what I wanted, and I hesitantly handed him the pack of cards. He disappeared in the back to read them while I sat in the front. I sat for what seemed an awfully long time, wondering. When I looked up and saw him coming, I tried to read the expression on his face, but couldn't. He looked at me sort of wondering, and asked if I could write a regular piece for them. So, I started publishing an occasional piece in the *Anvil*. But when I returned to Orangeburg for the 1970–71 term, there was no such organ as the *Anvil*; still I wanted to write. There was something that I wanted to say, but how and to whom? So, in the evenings I started to jot down my thoughts. As usual, I was regarded as odd, strange, and different.

I had a room in a house in town with two other women—an unhappy arrangement, since there was no heat in my bedroom. One night, therefore, when it felt chilly and damp, I went into the kitchen, where there was heat, closing the door behind me, to write. My housemates were in the living room, where there was a stove. After about an hour or so, one of the women opened the door and stared in. She wanted to know what I was doing. "Writing," I said. She plainly thought that I was out of my mind. But she closed the door and I continued. After about another hour, she left her companion again and flung the kitchen door open wide, firmly propping it. Clearly, there was not going to be any more subversive activity such as writing going on that night.

I stopped, but I had the rough draft of a piece comparing bus travel in the South before and after the Civil Rights Act of 1964. The next day I typed it up in the office on my Sears electric and put it away in a drawer.

Then one morning in late October—about six weeks later— I was looking at a "Today Show" interview, when Harrison E. Salisbury came on; he was being interviewed about the Op Ed Page, a new feature in *The New York Times*. When he said that he was reading unsolicited manuscripts, I decided to send him the bus piece, which I did that day. I didn't hear from the *Times* and decided after a while that the piece didn't meet their needs.

Christmas came and I went home to Durham for two weeks. When I got back to South Carolina State in early January and went to my box, there was a letter enclosing a clipping. *It was the bus piece!*

I knew a feeling that can only be described as wonder. I couldn't bear to read it. I just looked at it, with my byline and a brief note about me at the end. I carried it around all day and would occasionally take it out and look at it. Magic. I would start to read it—a few sentences at a time—then I would fold it up again. (It was about two days before I got to the end.)

That night I floated silently down, down, down in a warm, life-giving, life-sustaining gulf stream, rested on the bottom, and stayed there all night. Sleep, that fugitive, came back and became my steady companion. I didn't know it then but I had found what I had been seeking: *I was a writer.* Several pieces followed, and that June, while I was vacationing in New York, I went to the *Times* offices and met Harrison Salisbury and his staff. They were very warm to me.

We talked and, after what seemed like a few minutes, I looked at my watch—*45 minutes had passed*! I was embarrassed at taking up so much of Mr. Salisbury's time. And I said good-bye. But it wasn't good-bye at all. For as subsequent events proved, that morning I found a mentor, a confidant, and a friend.

Three months later I was in New York City again. It was Labor Day, 1971, a warm muggy Monday, and I was in the City because I was going to dinner at Harrison Salisbury's home that night. After checking into my hotel, I decided, as is my custom in New York, to wander along the streets and peer in windows, look at faces, and just enjoy myself in general. I walked in the Times Square area, always fascinating, and looked at the painted china, dwarf trees, and pictures that seemed to be painted layer on layer on mirrored surfaces. Passing a newsstand I decided to buy a *New York Times*, and, standing right there on the street, I started to thumb the pages. *And there it was!* A piece I had sent in on the civil rights movement and the black church. It was like a warm greeting to me, and in that vast, impersonal city, I felt immensely honored and pleased.

The dinner was lovely. The Op Ed Page staff and some of Mr. Salisbury's colleagues at the *Times* came. I waltzed on back to Durham, feeling like some of the literary figures I had read about who went "up" to London for various functions and then back to the provinces.

18

In the winter of 1971–1972 I lived at home in Wildwood with my mother and commuted to Chapel Hill, hoping to complete the writing of my dissertation. It was to be the last year of my mother's life.

It seemed to rain a lot after Christmas. I don't know if it really rained that much or if it was just my state of mind. The New Year, 1972, wasn't any better. The weather seemed dreary, without hope, as if spring were never coming.

I suppose it was the water continually dripping off the roof of the house that caused me to dream one night.

I was at the beach. The water was a clear greenish-brown close to the shore, but gray-blue farther out. In my dream it was early spring; the sun was mild in the late afternoon; in the morning, though, it was slightly chilly. It was off-season at the beach. It was uncrowded. Most of the beach houses looked boarded up. There were some hotels open, though, and some nice restaurants. I was happy; I loved the water. (I have often wondered about my love for the water, since I was born far inland and did not see the ocean until I was a teenager.) In my dream I made a transfer, remembering another time when I had seen the ocean. Then, it had been far, far away—a thin blue line on the horizon.

I was in Atlantic City the first time I saw the ocean. My father had died, and my mother took us—my younger brother and me—north to visit her sisters and brothers. One day we went to Atlantic City, but we never got to the ocean. The ocean was for white people. There was a section a long way away on the beach for "colored" people, but we didn't walk down that far. We walked on something called a boardwalk. We walked miles and miles, it seemed, in the hot sun, stopping now and then at a crowded place on the boardwalk to get a hot dog and a drink. But I didn't get to walk in the ocean.

Later when I read in books that excursions to the beach were supposed to be fun, gay and joyous, and that everybody was happy there, I smiled to myself; that day on the beach was one of the most miserable days in my life.

Aunt Marilyn was with us, and Aunt Marilyn was a drunk. She was married to my mother's brother, Uncle Bud. I was ashamed to be beside her. She was so obviously drunk and staggering, and she cussed like a sailor and didn't care who heard her—a squat little woman with a heavy black wig and dark glasses and a flowered dark-blue dress. Uncle Harry was drunk, too. He was the husband of Aunt Donna, my mother's baby sister. He looked bleary-eyed and grinned a lot, and he talked to Uncle Bud, who didn't say much: mostly he listened. Uncle Bud was rail-thin and very black, and he wore blue pants, a white sport shirt, and a round hat, a "porkpie," on his head. And they all talked and yelled—real loud. I was so ashamed, because we were a spectacle on the beach—everybody was looking. I couldn't really blame the people who were staring. Aunt Marilyn was drunk and cussing and acting every which way, and Uncle Harry was drunk and cussing but didn't act as bad as Aunt Marilyn. Uncle Bud had had a drink, but he was mainly trying to keep Aunt Marilyn from carrying on so bad.

"Rrrrr-ring . . . rrrrr-ring!" Aunt Marilyn's cussing was drowned out by the sound. I turned sleepily; there was a sharp noise in my ear. At first I ignored it; in my sleep I was still trying to see the thin gray line of the ocean at Atlantic City. It was far, far away. I wondered it I would ever reach it. The ring kept on. I thought that it was the alarm clock. I could tell that it was early in the morning. From far away I heard a voice; I couldn't be sure whether I was dreaming or not, because the voice sounded as though it was coming from another world—another planet. And the voice of Nonnie, my mother, said something about "collect," and "Germany," and "Jesse." Half-asleep and half-awake, I tried to put them together—"Germany". . . "collect" . . . and "Jesse." And then I came awake with a start. "No, operator, I will not accept the call," my mother said. She had the habit of repeating what the person on the other end of the line said, and had been saying the operator's words out loud.

My mother put the phone back on the hook and lay there for a while, very quiet. I knew what it must have cost her to say no. This was the first time in the more than twenty years since Jesse had left Durham to go into the Army, then had a long sojourn in New York City, then went back to the Army, that she had refused a collect call from him. The calls had come from New York City and from other places where he had been in the United States: the Deep South, East Coast, West Coast—everywhere. And, on two occasions, from Germany.

Nonnie dearly loved Jesse, that I was sure of. When he fell ill with pneumonia in Vietnam on his second tour of duty, she visibly shrank as telegram after telegram arrived from the Defense Department. The telegrams advised her to expect the worst. She sat under a tree on a Sunday afternoon as her friends came to visit her. She shed tears for the son who was being treated in Japan. Seemingly, she did not remember that he had gone for as long as three or four years without contacting her in any way.

My mother worried so much that I, desiring to help, to be a part of this family, decided to call Camp Zama, Japan, and see about Jesse. So, late one night I called, surprised that it took less than fifteen minutes to get through to the hospital. The nurse said, "Wait a minute, I'll go get him." In a few minutes Jesse was on the wire. I felt then that if he was ambulatory he was not going to die. The next morning, I was jubilant and rushed to tell Nonnie that I had talked to Jesse, that he could walk, had come to the telephone, and he had said a few words to me. To my hurt surprise, Nonnie did not thank me, and did not appreciate the fact that Jesse was no longer a subject for her tears and for her friends' commiseration.

I have sometimes wondered if Nonnie sensed that this year, 1972, was going to be the last year of her life—and if that was

212

what gave her strength to resist Jesse, just once. I'll never know, I suppose. I noticed, however, that after that incident she seemed to droop more and more.

It continued to rain a lot in February, and the troubles came just like the rain. My other brother, Ruf Junior, now sometimes called Ruf—like his father—was brooding, because he'd decided that he didn't have enough land. The land that my mother had given him for his house some fifteen years earlier still was uncultivated; only the plot that his house was on and the lawn around it had been attended to. But still he wanted more. He wanted more of the home place to make his share even with mine. He pressured her, and she gave in; but she had to ask my permission, because the house was in my name. Ruf did not know the house was in my name. Once he found out, he started to make war on my mother and me.

One Saturday night around midnight I heard a car door slam outside. I tensed. "Dear God, please don't let there be a row tonight." I waited to hear feet scraping on brick steps, then a door slam as Ruf went in his house, but I didn't hear that. Instead I heard feet scraping on cement steps—on our porch steps. He was coming to our house.

As a little girl I had watched my father build the forms and lay those cement steps. He had taken some wood and made a box, longer than it was wide. Once he had the hollow forms, Ruf Junior and I had put rocks and dirt in, and then my father plastered this over with cement; they were grand steps indeed.

And now Ruf was coming up those steps. He walked across the cement porch but I didn't hear his feet. This was the porch that had been poured after Hurricane Hazel blew away the wooden one in 1955. He put his body's weight against the door and pushed, and the door came open. I hated that very much—the fact that our house was really not secure. Both Ruf and Louise, his wife, kicked and pushed doors whenever they wanted to come in. They never knocked. Next I heard the long click, click, click of a number being dialed. The living room was in dim light. I had insisted that we have a dim light since my mother and I both got up during the night, and I thought it unwise to have us stumbling around in the dark when we could get a fifteen-watt bulb. My mother resisted at first, but once I bought the bulb and we used it for several nights, she wouldn't be without it.

My door opened to the living room; I was sleeping in Diane's old room. My mother's door was open; it opened into the little hall off the living room. Every sound in the house could be heard by my mother and me. There was no privacy. Ruf had stopped dialing; he was waiting for the party on the other end to answer.

"Whore!" he yelled.

I lay still. The yellow light from the small bulb in the living room caused furniture in my room to cast huge murky shadows on the wall. The two of us lay there listening. I could hear my mother in her room most of the time; the house was so small that lying on my bed I could even hear her when she turned the pages of a magazine.

"Slut."

The alcoholic abuse went on. What the quarrel was about, I was not able to determine. Ruf took delight in slamming the telephone down after each curse. Then he would carefully dial again, wait for the woman to answer, then call her another name and hang up again. My mother and I lay there in the dark, hearing each other breathe, wondering what would happen next and when the madness would cease.

I could only think thoughts that I had thought before: Merciful God, where are you? Why don't you put an end to all this? Why don't you just let him die in an auto crash? No, I mustn't think that. It is a sin to wish somebody dead. But, God, how much better off all of our lives would be if he were dead. Then Louise and the children could live in peace. Then my mother and I could live in peace, not having to listen to the falling furniture and the breaking glass, not seeing neighbors' lights flicker on in the dark, knowing that the madness had begun. What is the plan? Please show it to me. For I don't see it. There is something wrong in the universe. Some disjuncture, something that so far religion has never explained.

The intervals between the banging and the dialing had grown longer, and finally they ceased. I got my breath back again and lay there watching the dark murky shadow monsters on the wall until everything became quiet. Then I eased up to go look. Ruf was stretched out full-length on the sofa, sleeping. The room smelled of alcohol. He had come to let his enemies, my mother and me, know what he thought of us. Now he could sleep in our house and let us make of it what we would.

I eased the door shut. Tomorrow was Sunday. Somehow the nightmare would end. But when?

"Whore."

It was the next Saturday night. I was lying in bed. I guessed from the feel of the night that it was about midnight. In my sleep I had heard the car door slam. I heard feet on the cement steps—our house. Then there was knocking on the storm door; I had seen to it that it was locked tonight. My mother got up to let him in. Next I heard the sound when he picked up the receiver and started dialing. The nightmare had begun again.

I wondered who the woman was. He called her "Jetti." Why did she allow herself to be abused like that? But then perhaps she had made a mistake in getting mixed up with Ruf in the first place. She knew that he was married, and now she was anxious that no one know of her relationship with him. So she went along with this miserable game, hoping that he would soon tire of it. But he wouldn't tire of it, for he was not calling to punish the woman on the other end. He was calling to punish us. We were the "black bitches" of his wrath.

"Black whore."

Slam the receiver down. Pause. Dial again. Wait for the answer. Ruf knew from last week's experience that he had nothing to fear. I had not challenged him, and he need not worry about his mother.

Thus the dialing and the name-calling and the dialing went on and on, until about an hour later he tired of the game and went to sleep on the sofa.

The next day was Sunday, and people would pass by our white frame house set on a green lawn with a gigantic wisteria plant in front. And they would not know of the unchecked horror that reigned in there. I had read of early priests who went about exorcising evil. I was convinced that there was an evil spirit in our house. How else to explain the continuing nightmare of our lives?

Two weeks passed. Then one night the car door slammed again, and I braced myself. We were to get another inundation of filth. Why did we have to tolerate such behavior? I blamed myself for not leaving as soon as I heard the footsteps on the cement and the knocking at the door. Why did Nonnie let him in? But I knew why. Mother was afraid of him. Not of what he would do to her, but of what he might do to Louise. So she let him in, even though he had come to make the night horrid.

"Black slut."

I lay looking at the shadows on the wall, struggling for breath but trying to make no sound.

"Just a minute. I want my mama to talk to you."

I could have cried out at the viciousness of it. He didn't want the other woman to hear his mother; he wanted his mother to hear the other woman. He was saying to his mother: I spit on you and all you stand for. Not only would he bring knowledge of the other woman into his mother's house, but also he would force her to talk to the other woman, while next door his wife and three sons were in bed. Perhaps that would show them—his mother and sister—where they stood with him. He went into the bedroom.

"Get up," he said. "There's someone I want you to talk to."

"I don't want to, Ruf." She walked the short distance into the living room, and I heard her drag the foot that had never gotten over the stroke.

"Yes, you do. Here is the phone. Talk to the bitch."

216

"I don't want to. Leave me alone." Her voice was tired.

"Yes, you do. Here is the phone."

I lay in bed, unable to breathe. I was afraid to open my mouth, for I would start screaming.

"Hello." I heard her talking to the woman on the other end, whoever she was. She said a few polite words, and then I heard Ruf curse and slam the phone down. My mother stumbled in the dark, leaving the living room. She didn't fall against anything. Her leg gave way and she stumbled. I wanted to get up to see what was the matter. But then I knew that I would be drawn into it, and I didn't want that.

"Listen, bitch, you heard my mother." Ruf had dialed again. "I'm going to get her again. . . . Come on here, Mama, and talk to the bitch."

"Go on, Ruf, go on and leave me alone. Lord, have mercy."

"I said talk to the bitch."

"I want you to get out of my house. Right now."

From somewhere inside her she had summoned up some strength and had said what I had wanted her to say for so long.

I held my breath, and when the expected abuse started, I refused to listen. Had I listened, I would have grabbed something and tried to kill him. I wished again that he were dead, that he had died a thousand times.

The sound of the door closing and feet on the cement porch caused me to open my eyes. I listened, but I heard nothing. It was over. Soon I drifted off to sleep.

The next day was Sunday. My mother said, "You know, I feel bad today." That was the signal. Sometime during the night her indomitable spirit had started to fail, her strong heart had started to weaken.

I took her to Duke Hospital several times, and the doctor told me privately that her heart was failing and that nothing could be done. After several emergency-room and clinic visits, they admitted her.

The woman called Jetti eventually would file a complaint against Ruf Junior. As a result, he was found guilty and fined.

And the whole embarrassing story appeared in the Durham papers.

The tension was so great between Ruf and me that I went out of my way to avoid him when I visited my mother in the hospital. I went there in the mornings, figuring that Ruf would be at work. But each time a man's shadow passed the door where I was sitting, I couldn't breathe.

Then after another week had passed, I started visiting my mother in the nursing home to which Ruf had taken her.

Nonnie Mebane, like Ruf Senior, her husband, was a long time dying. She did not "go gentle into that good night." She raged, raged against the dying of the light and fought off death with every bit of strength she had. "Indomitable will" became to me more than cliché as I watched Nonnie struggle.

I never again visited her during "regular" times, but selected "odd" times when I was sure that no one else would be around. I was staying at Mason's Motel in Chapel Hill and trying to follow the "normal" pattern of a graduate student at the University. But my world was crashing all around me. It was Kafkaesque. And there was nothing I could do about it. I received some support from a Transactional Analysis group that was run by Bob Phillips, a Chapel Hill physician. But God seemed far away or, what is worse, uncaring.

Mother died in April. I had known the moment that she died. I was asleep on a Saturday afternoon, and suddenly I woke up, freezing cold. My teeth were chattering, and my body shook with chills. Though there was some chill in the air in the April mornings, in the middle of the day it was quite warm. So I was at a loss to understand what was happening to me. I got up and sat on the edge of the bed, wondering if I was very sick. Then, as suddenly as it came, the chill went. And in a few minutes I felt all right. Then the thought came to me: call. But I couldn't call. I might have had to listen to Ruf's voice, and I never wanted to hear it again. But still I wondered.

It was Saturday and I had not visited her since Friday, for I knew that I could never go to see her on Saturday or Sunday, when Ruf might be there. But I called anyway and Ruf told me that she was dead.

The few days surrounding my mother's funeral were surreal. I thought that if I could just make myself numb I could get through them. Nonnie's favorite expression was "I want everything to go along smooth," and I wanted this for her.

There was, however, talk of my not being permitted to attend the funeral. I stayed away from the house in Wildwood until the night before the funeral, when I knew the house would be full of people and thus safe for me. Other hands selected clothing and accessories for Nonnie's final rest.

The night passed. On the day of the funeral people were nervous and tense, but in the church we sat together as a family. I watched the proceedings but was not really there. I kept repeating to myself Nonnie's favorite phrase in life: "I want everything to go along smooth."

At the house, after the funeral and burial on the hill behind the church, people did not linger. I left before some of the out-of-town family. I had paid my last respects to Nonnie.

On a bright day in May I went to the house in Wildwood, crawled through the window on the front porch, and retrieved several things that were of value to me. I am sorry that I did not get the photographs that my mother always kept in her bureau drawer—of herself, my father, various relatives. But I was fearful and wanted to leave before my brother came back to his house next door. Mr. Don, who lived across the road, came over and "watched out" for me. Then I put the things in my car and fled the place where I was born and reared. There should be a more fitting close to such an important chapter in a human life, but this was the way it was for me.

I decided on this course of action after talking my options over with Sheriff McCloud, a black deputy. It seems that I had two. One: Take out a peace warrant against Ruf. Two: Get a permit—the sheriff would sign—and buy a gun. To me neither of these were viable options; violence would be held at bay, but not overcome. I couldn't live like that.

In midsummer 1972 I successfully defended my doctoral dissertation, which was on the North Carolina writer Charles W. Chesnutt. My graduate-school life was at an end, and I returned to my position at South Carolina State College in Orangeburg.

19

If writing was a warm and life-sustaining gulf stream—both writing itself and the people whom I met in connection with it—I could only dip into it infrequently. I still swam in a bitter sea of death-inducing salt and life-threatening carnivores.

First, I now had no family: no brother, aunt, uncle, or cousin wrote to me or called me or came to see me after my mother's death, and I must confess I am glad they didn't. Yet family meant a lot to me. To say that a person is without family is to say a very sad thing in human life. Diane, my niece, was now in the Murdoch Center for the mentally and physically handicapped near Durham. My profession didn't offer any joy either, for in trying to better my life I had started to produce work that was recognized *outside* the black community, and many blacks didn't like that. I was made aware of this on my return to South Carolina State, when at the first faculty meeting in late August 1972, the vice-president for academic affairs, near the end of his opening address, made a few offhand comments to the effect that writing was all right and nice, but not what South Carolina State was about. Everyone knew he was talking about me. He *knew* better, but he said it because there were those who had been at the College for a long time, had sinecures, had never published a line, and had no intention of doing so. If publishing reared its head as a criterion for the faculty, they would be lost. So the teachers wanted to scotch that right there, and the vice-president went along with them. People who wonder why black academics traditionally have been relatively unproductive of scholarship might ponder that situation.

There was, in addition, an episode with a man from the counseling center. He was new to Orangeburg, and he started coming to my office to see me, his excuse being that we "knew" some of the same people in North Carolina. The first time he came—all animated and gesticulating—I didn't think anything about it, but when his visits became rather frequent I began to wonder, for he never suggested that we have coffee or lunch or anything social.

After several weeks, he asked me to come to see his office. I demurred. An office is an office, and I didn't see any need to go out of my way to see one. Still he pressed me. I became uneasy and wondered out loud about it. He calmed me by saying that it was newly decorated. Still, I hesitated.

The next time he came, it was, "Come see my office" again. I told him I would take a different route to the post office one day and stop by to see it, which I did. He smilingly showed me around what was a very ordinary-looking office.

Then he suggested that I call him sometime. I knew that something was wrong; two and two weren't making four, but I couldn't figure it out.

Several days later I called him, and the secretary wouldn't let me speak to him. She insisted that I make an appointment to come in. I saw clearly that this "counselor" had misrepresented his "friendly" visits as professional ones and had led the counseling center personnel to believe that I was his *patient*. Then, to give his claim legitimacy in their eyes, he had to figure out a stratagem to get me to his office. But someone in charge wasn't satisfied and insisted that if I were indeed a patient, I should make an appointment and come in. I went to the dean of the faculty and made a formal complaint against this "counselor" and demanded that any records that he kept of his visits to my office be destroyed. He said that he would look into it. After that the counselor was careful to avoid me.

Then people who had been given a trip to New York City to attend the first—and, to my knowledge, only—meeting of the Black Academy of Arts and Letters stopped by my office to comment that, "We went to give the College some representation," meaning quite plainly that they, not I, despite my publishing in *The New York Times*, were the official literary representatives of the College.

Again I thought that I had better move on, but I didn't know where. I only knew that there were better people somewhere. There had to be.

I paused—pondering, "wondering, which way to go."

Late in mid-March of 1974, the answer came. The chairman of the English department at the University of South Carolina called. He had heard that I was planning to leave South Carolina State College. Before I left there, he said, I should come to Columbia to talk to him. (I knew the chairman, for I had taught one course a semester for two years in the evening division at the University of South Carolina.)

I went to see him and he made me a fine offer. It was mid-March. I remained undecided. I went to the dean of the faculty of South Carolina State and discussed the matter with him. I did not ask for more money, or for a reduced course load, only for a more considerate schedule (something I had requested for two years). Two full months passed and no counteroffer was made to me. On the final day of the term in mid-May I mailed in my resignation and left the state for the summer.

Living as I was in cultural and social isolation at South Carolina State, I had done one thing that saved me: at night I sat in my office typing, often until midnight or later. Scenes, pictures, and people of my childhood unfolded before my eyes, and I recorded them as they appeared. They flooded my consciousness—the sights, the sounds, the smells—all in color and three-dimensional. I heard the crickets cry at night—that dry, cracking sound—and I smelled the fresh cucumber/watermelonlike smell of a snake that has just shed its skin. And all so sharp and bright, I didn't see how I could capture the deluge. But I would try. When I was satisfied with something, I would send it to Mr. Salisbury. He would read it quickly and send it back, always with positive comments. By then I would have another passage ready to send. Sometimes, when I got home late at night, I couldn't go to sleep, for the people were still walking around and talking on that enormous movie screen in my head. So I would get up and write some more. Eventually I learned that if I wrote a humorous passage just before going to bed, I stood a better chance of falling off to sleep. But awake or asleep, I knew a real joy, for I was fulfilling my mission in life. That's how *Mary* was written and that is how I stayed alive at South Carolina State College. The bitter death-inducing brine of that environment drove me to seek, and eventually to find, the gulf stream of my life, writing.

What I remember most about Columbia, South Carolina, where I moved in the fall of 1974 when I accepted the offer from the University, is its cultural barrenness. This came as a surprise to me. I had lived in the Durham–Chapel Hill–Raleigh area (I didn't expect the arts to flourish in Orangeburg, South Carolina), where season tickets were a part of my life: to Broadway at Duke, The Carolina Playmakers, and Friends of the College, plus other attractions (speakers, performing artists, symposia). Therefore, I expected much more in a large city like Columbia. But except for lots of food places and what used to be called "honky tonks," many of them featuring local talent—"Home from Nashville"—there was relatively little of interest in the city.

In Columbia I observed a brutality in interpersonal relationships that shocked even me, and I thought that I had seen everything.

I heard a black professional male, unemployed and not looking for a job, tell a black professional woman who had been supplying him with food, shelter, and clothing for some time, "I've got bitches all over Columbia; I ain't never going to pay no rent." Though she was thirtyish and attractive, she took that from him. The reason: there are more professional-class black women in the city than men, and if she had told him to go, another black woman would have assumed her role immediately, and both of them knew it.

And a brutal murder in my neighborhood affected me so deeply that I wrote a piece about it which was published in *The New York Times*:

Vicki Got Wild Early

They carried Vicki Prideaux (not her real name) out in a plastic bag. She was a "good-time" girl and sometime during the night or early morning somebody cut her head off—hanging by a thread, people said. It was a good thing the children weren't home. She'd left them with neighbors.

They say she was a red-skinned girl who wore a tinted Afro-puff and that she wore her dresses short no matter how cold it got. She dressed for beauty.

She had a lot of men friends, but she left the women alone, except for one or two. Men kept things down; women talked from one to the other.

The men weren't boyfriends, though.

A lot of them were white. More money, you know.

But if she was your friend, you could count on her. If she had money, she'd give it to you, and if she didn't she'd pat her pocket and say, "I'll see you later on"—and she would.

Vicki should have slowed down. Women run in their 20's and early 30's, but by the time they're 34, like Vicki, they've started quieting down. But Vicki wouldn't slow down.

Vicki hadn't been too long out of the hospital. Someone stabbed her in front of the funeral home. They didn't know who; Vicki wouldn't tell. You know she always would get anybody told. She'd tell them exactly what was on her mind.

224

Saturday night she was probably drinking and started getting somebody told and he couldn't take it.

Vicki didn't have much of a chance. Her mother had ten or twelve children, most of them by different men. All of the children were good-looking, though. And Vicki got wild early. When she was sixteen she was arrested for spending the night in the barracks at Fort Jackson. Fifty dollar fine.

It was a shame to do her like that.

On the academic side, some unfortunate things happened to me at the University of South Carolina. My mentor and sponsor there, Dr. John R. Welsh, now promoted to vice-president for instruction, died suddenly one month after I arrived on campus. On the last Friday in September 1974, we had had a long interview in which he told me his plans for me at the University. After that interview, I felt that I had something to look forward to. But after his death the following week, I "fared but common" in the department.

I hung on by my fingernails and sheer grit as long as I could—about two and a half years—but when I saw that Dr. Welsh's plans for me were not going to be implemented, I decided to "let go and let God." Without a single faculty supporter and without anyone even saying good-bye, I left the University of South Carolina in May 1977. But I hung on in the city of Columbia, waiting, wondering what was going to become of me.

In my pain I wandered around, rode the buses, looked into store windows, sat at lunch counters, wondering. Sometimes as I walked at night I would clap my hands and sing a silent song, trying to hold back the fear and keep my spirits up. I remember walking and keeping time with my handclaps at Christmas as the lights on the small trees in front of the Bankers Trust tower glistened like human tears in the dark chilly night. I know that the drivers of the occasional cars that passed wondered who the woman was, walking along, seemingly self-engaged, in an hour when midtown Columbia was practically deserted except for the newsstand and the all-night restaurant next to it. I hoped that they didn't take me for Deborah, a deranged black woman, who at that time wandered through Columbia at all hours of the day and night, sometimes lucid but often completely disoriented.

The manuscript that became *Mary* I had submitted to publishing houses since the summer of 1972. Some saw possibilities, but none accepted it. I believe that *Mary* may have been ahead of its time. Although the sixties had passed, the *zeitgeist* of that decade lingered on in the early seventies, and *Mary* is not a sixties book. It is Southern, not Northern; it is small farm/small town, not urban; its characters are workers, not criminals or lumpenproletariat; they are churchgoers and rather conventional in their outlook, not "exotic."

Nothing happened; I was discouraged. So in the fall of 1974 I had shelved the manuscript in a closet in my apartment at Columbia, where it stayed for nearly three years. In the meantime Harrison Salisbury, on assignment for *Esquire*, came to the Deep South in November 1975. I gave a dinner for him and he interviewed me. (The interview appeared in *Esquire* in February 1976.) While he was in Columbia, he asked about the manuscript. In April 1976, during the spring break, I took it to New York for him to reread. He returned it in early summer with many encouraging comments. Still, I delayed doing anything for a whole year. Finally, in the summer of 1977, I mailed it off; this time it never returned, for while it was still in New York at one publishing house I saw in *The New York Times Book Review* the name of an editor whom I had met when he was visiting Chapel Hill in 1971. I wrote to him and he brought the book to the attention of The Viking Press.

The magical call came in September 1978. *They bought my book! I was going to have a book! Miracles do happen!* I still had months of waiting ahead, but from that moment on God has always seemed to be near. I don't doubt it at all.

The public library at the corner of Sumter and Washington streets was my refuge. Frequently I would make two trips a day there, during the day and again in the evening. It was a good way to kill time, and it was free. I would stay until the attendant started blinking the lights at ten minutes to nine. Since the Melrose Heights bus didn't make its stop across Sumter Street in front of the courthouse until nine-twenty, I had a twenty- to twenty-five-minute wait. At first I used to walk across Washington Street and sit in the Trailways bus station until quarter past and then go out to catch the bus, but I soon found it more fulfilling to wait for the bus hard by the Episcopal cemetery, across from the Banker's Trust tower. Sometimes, however, I would be too restless to sit and would keep walking, past the Carolina Townhouse, and would sit and wait for the bus across from the Methodist church near Barnwell.

One night when I got to this bench, there was a man sitting there.

"Mind if I sit down?" I said.

He moved to the right edge of the bench and indicated that I should have a seat. We talked about things that bus passengers usually talk about, like how long do you suppose it will be before the bus comes. Somehow the conversation turned to me, and he remarked that he had often seen me walking late at night—he himself usually got off about this time of night after completing his job as dishwasher in a midtown cafeteria. He told me that he often said to himself that that lady had better be careful.

Then he turned to me. "You *had* better be careful," he said. "It's dangerous to be out in this city so late." He was a heavy-set black man of about fifty years. His gentle voice contrasted so much with his physical form that it was startling.

I was so moved that someone had seen me and had cared what happened to me that I wanted to cry. Instead, I joked with him that I had better be careful talking to him—his wife or lady friend might see me and come up and jump on me. "No chance of that," he said, and laughed softly. I gathered then that he wasn't married and that there was no lady friend—I wondered about that, but did not comment.

Then I told him I had written a book. He wanted to know what it was about, and when I told him "my life," he said that he couldn't read or write, but that he would be sure to get a copy when it came out, and he wanted to know where he could buy it. I was amazed that he couldn't read or write, for he spoke so well, but I told him Belk's and he seemed to relax—probably because Belk's was a landmark in midtown and he knew where it was. By then the Melrose Heights bus was coming and we both boarded it.

During the next months, I would occasionally see him. If he had boarded the bus at Sumter and Gervais and I later in front of the church, we would throw up our hands to each other. Sometimes, however, I would grow tired of looking at the magazines and catch the eight-fifteen bus home or go out to Columbia Mall and sit and catch either an earlier or later bus back. Sometimes I simply would not see him for a long time.

One Saturday afternoon, however, in the dead of a South Carolina summer, when the one p.m. cable TV news frequently said, "High today in the low one hundreds," I saw my friend again. I didn't know it then, but that would be the last time I saw him. It was about three p.m. and he and one of the cooks were sitting outside in a shady spot on the wall around the rear parking lot of the cafeteria. They were taking a breather between the close of the lunch period and the start of the supper shift. For some reason I can't recall, I found myself taking a shortcut across the parking lot, and he called to me, introduced me to his companion, and told her that I had written a book. He wanted to know how it was coming along and again assured me that he was going to buy a copy when it came out. I went on my way, up the little steps that led to a parking lot, still marveling that someone who was illiterate could speak so well and conducted himself with such dignity.

Then one Sunday a story appeared in the *State* about the stabbing death of a man who was a dishwasher in a midtown cafeteria. The description fit my friend.

I inquired of the waitress if it was indeed the same man.

"Did he act kind of faggy?" she asked. "Killed over a bottle of wine and some money," she said, carefully removing items from the tray and setting them down without spills on the table. "You have to be careful who you take in." Her flat brown face with the carefully rouged lips didn't look up as she finished emptying the tray. "He didn't have to do all that."

She was talking about the man whom I knew and had come to regard in some ways as a friend. "He acted kind of faggy, didn't he?" she said.

I couldn't find words to respond to her. But then I realized what I had discovered more than once—that fine, compassionate people in an inhumane culture are not valued. Their compassion is thought soft or unmanly, their humaneness odd or feminine. My friend had taken in someone, befriended him, an argument had developed, and the object of his kindness had killed him.

He must have told me the night we met, but I never could remember his name.

And then one boiling hot day in late August 1980, I hailed a taxi to the Columbia airport and flew over a thousand miles to Milwaukee, Wisconsin. Dean William F. Halloran, a fair-minded, compassionate man, of the Division of Letters and Science at the University of Wisconsin–Milwaukee, had offered me an appointment. By now *Mary* was on the way, and I was arriving in another place to start a new life.

EPILOGUE

In March 1981, *Mary* was published; from the time advance proofs appeared, my life changed. It was excerpted in *Time* magazine in February 1981, and was reviewed in every part of the country. The reviewers were appreciative. Letters came in from readers in many parts of the nation and from some in foreign countries. They were a joy for me to read. Black readers said, "You have written down my life. I was born in such

229

and such a place and I remember we used to do such and such." Other ethnics with agrarian experience wrote that my book had recalled that for them. White ethnics who had neither the black experience nor the agrarian wrote that *Mary* had filled a gap in their understanding that they felt needed to be filled. And, a surprising number of black males wrote to say that they too had been discriminated against by other blacks because of their dark skins. A handful of letters came from people who had had troubled relationships with their mothers or fathers very similar to mine. These letters were special to me because they told me I was not alone in what I had thought was a singular situation.

My joy was wondrous. I remember going one Saturday to downtown Milwaukee and walking along Wisconsin Avenue, the main street of the city, just to look in the windows of the bookstores that displayed my book: Desforges, B. Dalton's, Schwartz. It was a dream.

Then, on a mildly chilly Christmas Eve, 1981, I visited my mother's grave on the little hill behind Mt. Zion Church in Wildwood. Diane was with me. And there in the North Carolina sunshine I made peace with Nonnie. The warfare was over.

Writing, the gulf stream of my life, had saved me. Now, I wish only to record the world around me as accurately and honestly as I can, until it is time to go and I lay down my pen.